Oscar Wilde, Parnellite Home Ruler
and Gladstonian Liberal

THOMAS WRIGHT is the author and editor of several Wildean books including *Oscar's Books* (Chatto, 2008; published in Vintage paperback in 2009 as *Oscar's Books: A Journey around the Library of Oscar Wilde*). Described by reviewers as an 'eccentric' 'bookshelf biography' it tells the story of Wilde's life through the books he read.

PAUL KINSELLA grew up in Ireland before moving to Canada in 1968. He completed a Ph.D. thesis on Wilde at the University of British Columbia in 2002 ('"We Must Return to the Voice": Oral Values and Traditions in the Works of Oscar Wilde'). Since 2007 he has been teaching full-time in the Liberal Studies Program at the British Columbia Institute of Technology.

Oscar Wilde, Parnellite Home Ruler and Gladstonian Liberal

Wilde's Career at the Eighty Club (1887–1895)

THOMAS WRIGHT & PAUL KINSELLA

© Thomas Wright and Paul Kinsella 2015–2024

This edition © 2025 Danaher Books (Oxford).
Revised from Thomas Wright and Paul Kinsella, 'Oscar Wilde,
a Parnellite Home Ruler and Gladstonian Liberal: Wilde's career at
the Eighty Club (1887–1895)', *The Oscholars* (August 2015).

All rights reserved. No part of this publication may be reproduced or
transmitted in any form or by any means, electronic or mechanical,
including photocopy, recording, or any information storage
and retrieval system, without permission in
writing from the copyright holder.

The right of Thomas Wright and Paul Kinsella to be identified as the
authors of the work has been asserted by them in accordance
with the Copyright, Designs and Patents Act 1988.

A CIP catalogue record for this book is available
from the British Library.

ISBN 978-1-0369-0723-5

Typeset in Equity A 10/13 by Rob Marland

Image credits: cover, Oscar Wilde by Sydney Prior Hall, 1888–1889 (NPG 2265); William Ewart Gladstone (1879) by Sir John Everett Millais (NPG 3637); Charles Stuart Parnell by an unknown photographer (LOC LC-B2-5620-13); Sketch of the Parnell Commission by Sydney Prior Hall (NPG 2250); back cover, Charles Stuart Parnell at the Parnell Commission by Sydney Prior Hall (NPG 2229); others, authors' collection.

Contents

Preface • vii

Introduction • 1
Wilde joins the Eighty club • 4
Why did Wilde join the club? • 10
Wilde's early views on Irish politics • 13
Wilde's early views on English political parties • 27
Wilde's reaction to Tory coercion • 31
The Parnell Commission • 34
An active Eighty Clubber • 42
Parnell's downfall • 49
A disillusioned Home Ruler; still a recalcitrant patriot • 53
Wilde's downfall and the Eighty Club • 56

Appendix: Timeline • 61
Works cited • 65
Notes • 71

Preface

IN THE EARLY 2000s, I was at the Clark Library in Los Angeles, researching Oscar Wilde's Tite Street library for my monograph *Oscar's Books* (2008). While I was examining a slim pamphlet that had once belonged to Wilde, entitled *The Eighty Club 1890*, a piece of paper fell from its pages onto my desk. It was a receipt, dated 26 April 1889, for Wilde's payment of annual membership dues to the Eighty Club, a Liberal party organization founded in 1880 for the promotion of Liberalism in Britain.

I realised that the secondary Wildean literature included no references to Wilde's membership of this political club, so I decided to investigate Wilde's links to it. My research was carried out mainly at Oxford's Bodleian Library, which houses an archive dedicated to the Eighty Club, and also offers access to contemporary newspapers. Over the ensuing years I discovered a great deal about the purpose, composition, and activities of the Liberal organization, as well as about Wilde's membership, which spanned the years 1887–1895, and involved his attendance and participation at club events. I learned that, after 1886, the Eighty Club was engaged in the advancement of specifically Gladstonian Liberal causes, most notably the promotion of Home Rule for Ireland, which would have granted Wilde's native country a measure of self-government within the United Kingdom. Consequently, I sensed that Wilde's decision to join the organization in 1887 might have significant implications for our understanding of his attitudes to Irish Home Rule, and to Irish Nationalism and British politics generally.

In 2012 I wrote about my findings in a 5000-word journalistic essay, which was eventually published in *The Times Literary Supplement* (UK) in 2014, under the title: 'Party political animal: Oscar Wilde, Gladstonian Liberal and Eighty Club member' (the essay was then long-listed for Notting Hill Editions' William Hazlitt Essay Prize in 2016). Soon after completing that essay, I approached my friend, the Wilde scholar Paul Kinsella, and invited him to work with me on a much longer, scholarly paper, with the idea of presenting it at a conference, and publishing it in an academic journal. Between 2013 and 2014 we worked together on a paper which was presented by Kinsella at the 'Wilde in Paris 2014' conference chaired by D.C. Rose, and entitled 'Not Mentioned in Despatches: Some New Evidence on Oscar Wilde's Participation in Politics'.

After the conference we compiled our scholarly paper. At 15,000 words (plus around 14,000 words of endnotes) it was far too long to submit to an academic journal; in any case, we were keen to draw on the editorial and Wildean expertise of D.C. Rose, editor of the *Oscholars*, so we approached Rose with the idea of publishing the essay on his site. Rose accepted the essay and, after various revisions had been made, it was published on 3 August 2015, under the title 'Oscar Wilde, a Parnellite Home ruler and Gladstonian Liberal: Wilde's career at the Eighty Club (1887–1895)'. On 8 September 2015, we published a revised version of the essay, which took into account some readers' suggestions and corrections.

Over the next few years, our *Oscholars* essay was read and cited by Wilde scholars, such as Geoff Dibb, Noreen Doody, Richard Haslam, Jarlath Killeen, Matthew Sturgis, and Mark Turner. Unfortunately, however, a couple of years ago, the *Oscholars* website (http://www.oscholars.com) went offline, rendering the essay inaccessible. We have recently placed our original essay on some alternative sites.[1]

We have also decided to publish the essay in this pamphlet form, to ensure its continuing accessibility and survival into the future, following the advice of Robert Darnton: 'anyone who wants to preserve a digital work [should] print it on paper'.[2] In addition, we wanted to make further revisions to it. Although we have found no evidence to alter the general conclusions arising from our original research, we have clarified and amplified some expressions, and made numerous stylistic changes. We have added references to Wilde's attendance at three Eighty Club meetings that we didn't mention in our 2015 essay; these were recently brought to our attention by Rob Marland. We also feel it is fitting to publish in palpable form an essay that owed its inspiration to the serendipitous appearance of the slip of paper which fell out of that pamphlet in the Clark Library over twenty years ago.

We would like to take this opportunity to thank the editors and expert Wildean readers who have commented on our work (in any of its incarnations): Bruce Bashford, Davis Coakley, Geoff Dibb, Noreen Doody, Sos Eltis, Adrian Hardiman, Alan Jenkins, Jarlath Killeen, Rob Marland, D.C. Rose, Horst Schroeder, Ian Sheehy, Philip E. Smith II, Matthew Sturgis, Heather White, and John Wyse Jackson.

Thomas Wright, Genoa
Paul Kinsella, Vancouver
November 2024

Introduction

THIS ESSAY OFFERS a full account of our findings concerning Oscar Wilde's membership of the Eighty Club, a Liberal political organization founded for the promotion of Liberalism within the House of Commons and among the British electorate.[3] Its aim is to present, contextualize and analyse our findings and their implications for Wilde's political activities and opinions. When the record of Wilde's eight-year membership (from 1887 to 1895) is set in the wider context of his political statements and writings concerning the so-called Irish question and his multifarious nationalist activities, it becomes clear that he publically identified himself with the cause of Parnellite Home Rule for Ireland. The combined weight of specific and contextual evidence also suggests that, from the late 1880s to the early 1890s, Wilde adopted the public persona of a party political animal, alongside all the other roles he performed in the period, such as author, journalist, socialite and raconteur.

The essay shows that the trajectory of Wilde's involvement with the Eighty Club was marked by key turning points, in 1887, 1891–1892 and 1895. By joining the club in 1887, Wilde publically declared his approval of the position on Irish constitutional independence arrived at by William Gladstone in the winter of 1885–1886, when the Liberal leader had converted to the Home Rule cause and subsequently formed an alliance with Charles Stewart Parnell's Irish Parliamentary Party (IPP). Between 1886 and 1887, the Eighty Club's centre of gravity had lurched towards Gladstone's new Irish policy, so 1887 was an opportune moment for a Parnellite Home Ruler such as Wilde to nail his colours to the Gladstonian Liberal mast.

Wilde participated in the Eighty Club's political and social events from 1887 until the summer of 1892. His interest in the club appears to have waned by that time, when he attended his last Eighty Club gathering. After mid–1892, we have no evidence of his involvement in the club's activities. It is, we believe, no coincidence that Wilde's disengagement from Liberal political activities occurred between the end of 1890 and the summer of 1892, as it was the period of Parnell's disgrace and downfall, in the wake of the O'Shea divorce scandal and the split of the IPP. During this time, Gladstone cut Parnell adrift and the prospects of achieving Home Rule through English party politics significantly receded. We think it highly likely that Wilde was disillusioned by these developments.

In 1895 Wilde's membership of the Eighty Club was rescinded by the committee for non-payment of subs. This was, of course, the year of Wilde's own downfall. We will describe and explore the surprising and influential role prominent Eighty Club members played in orchestrating Wilde's arrest and conviction.

Our essay begins with two short sections, which aim to set the scene. 'Wilde joins the Eighty Club' offers a brief description of the club, and of the immediate political context in which Wilde decided to join it; the second section ('Why did Wilde join the club?') explores the possible reasons he became a member. We believe Wilde's motivation was primarily political, and that this can best be understood from a wider perspective on his political thinking. Consequently, in the two sections that follow, we turn our attention to Wilde's views on the 'Irish question', and also to his attitude to English party politics, up to 1886. The titles of these sections are: 'Wilde's early views on Irish politics' and

'Wilde's early views on English political parties'. In the former we elucidate and contextualize Wilde's opinions on Ireland in detail in an attempt to do justice to their complexity and importance. We also quote generously from a Wilde interview from 1882 that is unfamiliar to most Wilde scholars. A third background section, 'Wilde's reaction to Tory coercion', describes the nationalist views Wilde expressed from 1887 onwards in his journalism and literary works, as well as in an 1887 speech he made to an Irish literary club.

Having established fully the context of Wilde's decision to join the Eighty Club, we are in a position to offer an account of his eight-year membership. In our chronicle of the active years of Wilde's membership (1887–1892) his club activities are placed alongside his other Home Rule activities and statements, to form one overarching narrative of commitment to the Home Rule cause. As Wilde's engagement with the club decreased around 1891–1892, we focus exclusively on his nationalist statements in the next chronological section, covering the years 1891–1895. In the final section, 'Wilde's downfall and the Eighty Club', we examine the end of Wilde's club membership in 1895, and the club hierarchy's complicity in his imprisonment.

A timeline of Wilde's Eighty Club and nationalist activities is provided in an appendix (and readers may wish to refer to this as they go through the essay). This shows the clear relationship between the Gladstonian and Parnellite lines of Wilde's nationalist political engagement – lines that were intertwined for the four-year period 1887–1891.

Wilde joins the Eighty Club

IN 1887 OSCAR Wilde joined the 'Eighty Club', an all-male Liberal Party organization which had been formed shortly before the general election of 1880 (hence its name).[4] The club's objectives were 'to bring together successive generations of Liberals, with a view to the promotion of the Liberal cause in the House of Commons and at Parliamentary Elections' and 'promoting Liberal Education, and ... stimulating Liberal organization in the country'. The necessity 'for some such body was felt in consequence of the numerous applications received by the Central Association of the Liberal Party for the assistance of Speakers and Lecturers at meetings'.[5] Prominent young Liberal politicians such as Herbert Henry Asquith and the Earl of Rosebery were on the committee; the club President was William Gladstone who, at the time Wilde joined, had been Prime Minister three times.

In its first two years the club had around fifty members, but by 1886 its ranks had swollen to five times that number. At that time Liberal MPs made up roughly fifteen percent of the membership (around the same number of club members had tried, but failed, to gain seats at the 1886 general election). Most members were Liberal journalists, solicitors and socialites young enough to join, candidates having to be less than forty years of age.

As well as supplying speakers at Liberal meetings throughout England, the Eighty Club hosted its own political and social events. It organized talks in public venues and held formal dinners at which MPs gave speeches on the important political and party-political issues of the day. A few months after these speeches were delivered, the club published them in pamphlet form, often inside the club's annual report, but sometimes separately. Less formal club 'conversaziones' were held in London hotels, at which members smoked and circulated before MPs spoke. There were, in addition, informal social events known as club 'at homes', where aristocratic members would open the doors of their London residences to fellow Eighty Clubbers. Members could bring along both male and female guests to many of these events.

Wilde joined the club at a turning point in its history. Gladstone's conversion to the cause of Home Rule in the winter of 1885–1886, and his subsequent alliance with Charles Stewart Parnell's IPP and decision to introduce a Home Rule Bill, had sent tremors through the Liberal Party. A substantial group of Liberals opposed their leader's new policy on Ireland. These dissidents, composed of members of the Whig faction of the party (many of whom were influential grandees with land in Ireland) and numerous Liberal Radicals, such as Joseph Chamberlain, were dubbed 'dissentient' Liberals at the time, but they would eventually become known as the Liberal Unionists. The Liberal Unionists voted against Gladstone's 1886 Home Rule Bill, which proposed that a newly created Irish Parliament control taxation and other spheres of government (with the exception of such things as foreign policy, defence, and religion, in order to ensure the 'integrity of the Empire'), and which also gave tenants the opportunity to purchase land, at a price generous to landlords, with credit provided by the British Government. When the bill was defeated at its second Commons reading in June 1886, Gladstone's government resigned and a general election was called. The election was effectively a referendum on the 'Irish question', now the defining issue of English party politics. During the campaign Tories such as Lord Randolph Churchill stirred up anti-Home Rule sentiment in England and among the Protestant minority in Ulster, coining the slogan 'Ulster will fight, and Ulster will be right!' and arguing that Home Rule would effectively mean 'Rome Rule'. The UK electorate rejected Home Rule, with the Tories and the Liberal Unionists (who made the tactical decision not to contest the same seats) winning a majority of 118 over the combined forces of the Gladstonian Liberals and the IPP. The Tories then formed a government, under the leadership of Lord Salisbury, which was propped up by their new Liberal Unionist friends.

The schism within the Liberal Party was replicated within the Eighty Club. At first the organization had endeavoured to preserve unity by deciding, at a Special General Meeting on 21 June 1886, 'to take no part in the General Election ... in order to avoid division [between Gladstonians and Unionists]'. The central ground could not hold, however, and things fell apart in the summer of 1887 when the organization officially aligned itself with the Gladstonian Liberals by declaring it 'the duty of the Liberal Party to maintain and enforce the policy of Home Rule'. In protest, eighty Liberal Unionist club members resigned. Soon afterwards, at a general club meeting held on 29 June 1887, eighty candidates awaiting election to the club were recruited to fill their places. It is likely that Wilde was one of these candidates, because around 80% of the new members recruited in 1887 via an ordinary club election were elected on this occasion. Wilde was one of 112 new recruits for the year who swelled the club's membership by around a third to 310 members, the largest number in its history. Because of the split within the club (and party) over Irish policy, all of these new recruits were, by definition, committed Home Rulers and staunch Gladstonians. In taking its hard line on Home Rule, the Eighty Club proved itself to be the most dogmatic and ardent of the London Liberal clubs, the organization allowing its

William Ewart Gladstone (1879) by Sir John Everett Millais. Wilde pronounced the portrait 'one of the great pictures of this century'.

members less 'individual freedom of political opinion' on the issue than sister institutions such as the National Liberal Club. In 1887, when the Eighty Club was officially endorsing Home Rule, the National Liberal Club passed 'a resolution directed against the Club taking an active part in politics, and emphasizing the claim that it was a Club of the whole Party'. Although the Liberal Unionists did eventually resign en masse from the National Liberal Club they did not do so until the winter of 1888–1889 – a whole year and a half after they had been forced to leave the Eighty.[6]

In the very year Wilde joined, the Eighty Club was thus transformed into the intellectual and social heart of Gladstonian Liberalism, a political movement now defined, to a considerable extent, by its support for the Home Rule cause. Promising young politicians loyal to Gladstone dominated club and committee; the club became a think tank for Irish policy and an organ for the diffusion of Home Rule propaganda. From 1887 onwards it organized numerous meetings with a Home Rule theme. In addition, it published *The Eighty Club Circular*, a newspaper sent out to club members and sold to the public, which aimed 'to instruct the English electorate in Irish history' as a 'means of promoting Home Rule policy', and to inform them of 'the actual state of things existing in Ireland, and the real character of the Coercion Act'.[7]

The Coercion Act was introduced in August 1887 by the Tories, with the support of many Liberal Unionists, with the aim of giving the Tory Chief Secretary of Ireland, Arthur Balfour, the weapons to fulfil his brief of 'restoring order' to Ireland (rural agitation had returned to the country, after the failure of the 1886 Home Rule Bill, in the form of the 'Plan of Campaign').[8] Under the provisions of the act Balfour could condemn as illegal any group of protesters, and try, without jury, anyone arrested on the charges of intimidation and non-payment of rent. With the help of the Irish Unionist barrister Edward 'Coercion' Carson, 'Bloody Balfour' secured the convictions of numerous Irish political leaders and Home Rule campaigners – William O'Brien, and the English poet and Home Ruler Wilfrid Scawen Blunt among them.

The year 1887 was one of heightened passions and divisions, not only between English rulers and Irish subjects, but also within the British body politic, over how to deal with the now unavoidable presence of the 'Irish question'. To those with a keen interest in the issue, and who advocated a particular policy, it seemed like a decisive period, when a great deal was hanging in the balance. It was a time to lend weight and support to the cause one espoused, a time when a statement or action defined one's position distinctly (e.g. the poet and critic Matthew Arnold, the poet Algernon Charles Swinburne and the Poet Laureate Alfred, Lord Tennyson publicly opposed the 1886 Home Rule bill, and two new London Unionist clubs – the Junior Constitutional and the National Union – were founded in 1887). Wilde chose this moment to join a club that was in the process of redefining itself along pro-Home Rule, anti-coercion and Gladstonian lines.

Why did Wilde join the club?

THERE ARE SEVERAL non-political reasons why Wilde might have joined the Eighty Club. He may have viewed membership as part of his ambitious social networking campaign, or as an excellent chance for meeting the educated, well-to-do young men in whom he was interested, socially, romantically and sexually. London clubs appealed to many men who were attracted to men. They provided a congenial homosocial environment and offered, in Nicholas Frankel's words, 'a way for unmarried gentlemen to enter the legitimate social sphere'.[9] It is hardly surprising that some members of the Eighty Club were known, or rumoured, to be men who loved men (such as Lord Rosebery, Viscount Drumlanrig and Reginald Turner). As a budding journalist too, desperate to make a splash and some cash, Wilde may have seen the club as a promising hunting ground for contacts and commissions. The editors of the OUP edition of Wilde's journalism emphasize the 'clubbableness' of the newspaper community at this time, and suggest that journalists needed access to London's clubs to get ahead as well as to remain 'au courant'.[10] We know that in 1887–1888 Wilde joined (or tried to join) other London clubs which offered similar professional and social opportunities, such as the Savile and the Society of Authors. That said, the Eighty Club ranked lower, in social terms, than elite Liberal clubs such as the Reform and Brooks's, while the limited size of its membership, and the fact that it had no permanent home, meant it offered fewer opportunities (social and professional), and made it far less attractive as a meeting place than, for example, the National Liberal Club.[11]

It is more commonsensical to suggest that Wilde's principal motive for becoming a member of an overtly political club was political. The club's uncompromising attitude to its Liberal Unionist members in 1887 reveals its dogmatic ethos, while its official aims and rules emphasize its explicitly political character as well as the high level of engagement and activism expected from members. A candidate for the Eighty declared himself willing to carry out 'political work for the party' and, 'at the end of each year to send to the club Secretary information as to the political work done by him'. (Among other things, the club expected members to be 'willing to give voluntary assistance by speaking at public meetings and by delivering lectures on political subjects' at Liberal meetings throughout the country).[12] This rule had to be strictly adhered to, as 'any member who has failed to do sufficient work to justify membership, shall cease to be a member'. From the outset then, the thirty-three-year-old aesthete, who sometimes enjoyed posing in public as flippant, would have been aware of the vital importance of being an active and earnest espouser of the Liberal cause.[13]

As we have suggested, Wilde's decision to join the Eighty Club in 1887 is eloquent of a commitment to the Home Rule cause, and also evidence of a willingness to publically identify as a Gladstonian Liberal. It is significant in this context that Wilde would attend numerous Eighty Club events with a specifically Home Rule theme, and was the designated speaker at one of these. It is equally telling that, concurrently, he was engaged in nationalist activities outside the club – attending other Home Rule political meetings, signing Home Rule petitions, and making his views on Irish issues clear in his journalistic writings and during newspaper interviews. Full details of these activities are provided in the narrative account of Wilde's Eighty Club career and nationalist activities below. However, before offering that narrative, it is necessary to provide further context regarding Wilde's decision to join the Eighty Club, in order to understand fully the motivation and significance of that decision.

Wilde's early views on Irish politics

AS AN OXFORD undergraduate Oscar Wilde voiced opinions on Irish politics that were, according to an English acquaintance, animated by a 'strong feeling against England', which he had inherited 'from his mother, a violent nationalist.'[14] The variety of nationalism Wilde inherited from 'Speranza' (as his mother had styled herself in her youth) was indeed strong, yet complex and ambiguous in certain respects.

In the late 1840s Speranza had become, through her poetry, the spokeswoman for the nationalist Young Ireland group, whose writings inspired what Wilde referred to as 'our unfortunately unsuccessful rebellion of '48'. During that failed revolution nationalists had taken to the streets in an attempt to wrest control of their country back from the English, whose monarchs had claimed technical overlordship of Ireland from the twelfth century, and personal overlordship since the time of Henry VIII, and who had formally subsumed Ireland into the United Kingdom in 1800. Speranza trained the young Wilde to 'love and reverence' the writers of the Young Ireland movement, 'as a Catholic child [reverences] the Saints of the Calendar.' An 1863 edition of Speranza's verses is dedicated to 'my sons Willie and Oscar Wilde' with the following words: 'I made them indeed / Speak plain the word COUNTRY. I taught them, no doubt, / That a country's a thing one should die for at need.'[15]

In addition, Speranza wrote journalism and books on the politics, history and folk legends of Ireland. In these writings she often advocated the restoration of some kind of political autonomy to Ireland, through the repeal of the 1800 Act of Union, which had abolished the Irish parliament and forced Irish MPs to sit at Westminster. She also espoused the cause of Land Reform, which aimed to help Ireland's Catholic tenantry and peasantry. Throughout her prose works, Speranza was unrelenting in her criticism of the Anglo-Saxon race, which she characterized as stupid, docile and materialistic, and fulsome in her praise of the intellectual, altruistic, passionate and ethereal 'Celt' (her son would espouse similar racial opinions).

Her firebrand views notwithstanding, Speranza, and her husband Sir William Wilde, were members of Ireland's Anglo-Irish Protestant governing caste, which had strong political, genealogical, cultural and religious ties to England. Wilde described his mother as growing up 'in an atmosphere of alien English thought, among people high in Bench and Senate far removed from any love or knowledge of those wrongs of the people [i.e. the Catholic tenantry and peasantry] to which she afterwards gave such passionate expression.'[16] (Wilde's own education at Portora, one of the Royal Schools of Ulster, and at Trinity College was, likewise, of an English and Protestant variety). The Wildes were part of the professional Protestant middle-class élite (Sir William was a prominent Dublin doctor and Speranza a journalist) rather than an old Anglo-Irish landowning family of aristocratic status. Nevertheless the family did own land in the west of Ireland and multiple properties which they rented out. Sir William indeed hoped that by purchasing land and property he might elevate the Wildes from the ranks of professional people into those of the country gentry.[17]

Because of their background and social status, the Wildes had very little in common with the Catholic peasantry and tenantry who made up the bulk of Ireland's population. Although they were of Ireland, the Anglo-Irish caste were regarded by many Catholics – at least by the second half of the nineteenth century – as not truly Irish.[18] In their myriad writings, on archaeology, politics, literature and ancient history, the Wildes attempted to overcome the social and religious divide by celebrating, and attempting to forge, a sense of national Irish identity strong and capacious enough to unite the Protestant élite and the Catholic Irish peasantry.[19] The Wildes' decision to publish three collections of Irish folklore was partly inspired by the same political aim.[20]

As members of the Anglo-Irish élite it is hardly surprising that the Wildes' political views were patrician, paternalistic and in some respects conservative. Sir William had opposed the Young Irelander's uprising, and, while favouring the restoration of Ireland's eighteenth-century parliament, he does not seem to have ever advocated the idea that Ireland should leave the British Empire (on this point, Speranza was also sometimes ambivalent).[21] Speranza was pleased William received a knighthood from the Queen, and she was happy to accept the pension solicited for her from Victoria some years after her husband's death in 1876. She disliked the idea of an Irish government elected by the majority Catholic peasantry and dominated by representatives from their ranks – 'a rude, uncultured mob'.[22] Likewise, notwithstanding her incendiary verse, and her friendship with Fenians such as John Mitchel (whom both she and Oscar publically praised) Speranza was emphatically 'not a Fenian'. The Fenians belonged to revolutionary republican groups, such as the Irish Republican Brotherhood, who rose up against British rule in Ireland in the 'doomed rebellion' of 1867 (but who would, in 1916, help direct the far more momentous Easter Rising). Speranza disliked the fact that Fenians came from all social classes: 'it is decidedly a democratic movement', she wrote to a friend,

'& the gentry and aristocracy will suffer much from them!' While Speranza often advocated the formation of a republican government she was appalled by the possibility that Ireland would become a 'Fenian Republic'.[23]

The emergence, and growing momentum, of a popular Catholic nationalist political movement in the nineteenth century, first under the 'Liberator' Daniel O'Connell, and then under groups such as the Fenians, was a threat to the Anglo-Irish caste (as was the increasing prominence of the Catholic middle-class in professions formerly dominated by the Ascendency). The establishment of an independent Irish democracy would sound their death knell as a governing class. Some members of the caste embraced nationalism, in the hope that by placing themselves 'in the van of a national cultural revival', they might exert some influence over events and perhaps even guarantee their own survival.[24] The motives of many Anglo-Irish nationalists were therefore ambiguous, just as their views were equivocal and multifarious.

Despite the ambivalence and haughtiness of her views, Speranza can be placed at the radical end of the Anglo-Irish nationalist spectrum, because of the choices she made in the late 1870s in response to the evolving political situation. The Dublin barrister Isaac Butt, well known to the Wilde family, had established the Home Rule League (aka the Home Rule Party) in 1873. A conservative Anglo-Irishman, Butt campaigned for a modification of the Act of Union through the establishment of an Irish parliament that would still be subordinate to England and part of the Empire. Butt gained the support of many Anglo-Irish Protestants, yet aroused the suspicions and ire of some Catholic nationalists and Fenians, such as John Mitchel, who demanded far more aggressive tactics and ambitious aims. Such demands placed Butt in an impossible position – as Catholics formed the bulk of both the Irish electorate and his party's membership he

Charles Stuart Parnell by an unknown photographer

was compelled to respond, yet under no circumstances would he betray his Anglo-Irish caste.

Nevertheless the movement grew as a parliamentary force – more than sixty Irish Home Rule members were elected to the Westminster parliament between 1873 and 1877. One of these was Parnell, an aristocratic land-owning Anglo-Irish Protestant from Co. Wicklow who espoused more radical views than Butt, even implying at times some Fenian sympathies. Over the next few years Parnell would transform the Home Rule movement into a potent force which genuinely represented Catholic as well as Protestant Ireland. He became chairman of the Home Rule Party in 1880 and, two years later, re-branded it as the Irish Parliamentary Party (IPP). In altering the movement's direction and ethos Parnell may have been motivated by a strong antipathy to England inherited from his Republican American mother; he also seems to have believed that constitutional and land reform might deliver a decent deal to his Anglo-Irish caste, and even bring them into the nationalist fold. He was, in addition, inevitably responding to events. The potato crop failure of the late 1870s, and falling prices, politicized the Catholic tenantry and peasantry; this led to the formation of the Land League in 1879. The league was the organized political expression of Irish rural discontent. Michael Davitt was one of its founders; Parnell became its President.

Historians speak of the 'polarizing' of Irish politics in the late 1870s and early 1880s and the 'plebianizing' and 'radicalization' of the Home Rule movement.[25] Many Anglo-Irish landowning Protestants washed their hands of the nationalist cause, Parnell being one of the very few (if not the only one) prominent in the Land League. Some members of the caste actively campaigned against Home Rule, forming the Irish Loyal and Patriotic Union which advocated the preservation of the Union. The IPP was now increasingly dominated by members of the professional Catholic middle-class.

In her pamphlet *The American Irish*, written towards the end of the 1870s, Speranza made her position on these developments clear: 'the regeneration and re-creation of Ireland will not come through Home Rule as understood by its present supporters and leaders [i.e. Butt and conservative Anglo-Irish nationalists] if, indeed, that hollow fiction is not even now almost extinct. [Buttite] "Home Rule," with its old feudal distinctions of class and caste, is looked upon with bitter disdain by the advanced party in Irish politics [i.e. that of Parnell and perhaps Davitt], and it will never be galvanised into life again by any amount of platform platitudes. A National Convention, with supreme power over all that concerns Ireland, and control of the revenues, to be composed of members elected by universal suffrage, and secured in power for a definite time, is the idea most prominently set forth … . The new movement will have a larger and more comprehensive aim than the mere "Repeal of the Union." … The new wine must be poured into new bottles…'.[26] Speranza's advocacy of universal suffrage here is striking.

Speranza's son appears to have followed the changing political situation with interest. Wilde described *The American Irish* as an 'extremely … interesting political prophesy' animated by 'fire and enthusiasm', and also 'part of the thought of the nineteenth century'.[27] On 24 May 1877 he attended a meeting of the Catholic University Literary Society and the Historical Society, at which the 'formation of an Irish National literature' was discussed by prominent authors and politicians.[28] In December 1877 he penned an appeal in *Saunders' News-Letter* that resonates with nationalist views, in which he solicits public financial support for the painter, art historian and Home Ruler Henry O'Neill, whose work, he says, is characterised by an 'unselfish patriotic devotion to Ireland'.[29]

At the same time, Wilde was attempting to establish himself as a poet and critic in England, an environment that was often

A NARROW ESCAPE.

'A Narrow Escape', a cartoon by George du Maurier for *Punch* (9 April 1881, p. 158) in which an Irish landlord returns to England after visiting Ireland. 'We have missed you!' says a young woman. 'So have my Tenants, thank goodness!' the landlord replies. The man at left, with long hair and a fur coat, resembles Wilde.

hostile to Irish nationalist aspirations, as well as to Irish culture, and the Irish themselves. It was perhaps for this reason that Wilde attempted to eliminate his Irish accent while studying at Oxford University (which was effectively brain of the British Empire, since many of its graduates filled administrative positions in the colonies); and that Wilde also, on occasion, advertised the English side of his cultural heritage, even implying, at times, that he was English (in a sonnet, about the grave of John Keats, composed in the late 1870s, Wilde wrote of 'our English Land', and in a lecture penned in 1881–1882 he spoke of 'our

English renaissance'). The idea that such opportunistic pronouncements were tinged with immigrant anxiety is supported by the testimony of Robert Sherard, who knew Wilde as a young man, as well as in his later years. '[Wilde] was,' Sherard commented, 'proud of being an Irishman, very proud... he was always keen to assert, even as a boast, the fact that he was an Irishman ... [but] Irishmen and Irish matters were not popular in his day in the London Society to which he aspired; and though he never denied his nationality *before he had arrived*, he took particular care not to let it transpire.' (Our italics.)[30]

It was during his 1882 lecture tour of America that Wilde was most vocal in his support for the nationalist cause. This is unsurprising, because of the keen interest in Irish politics shown by the large Irish-American community in the country, whose views were often of a radical nationalist cast. When Irish leaders such as Parnell visited the country and addressed Irish-American audiences the rhetoric they used was usually more radical than the rhetoric they used in England. This factor should not be forgotten when reading the political statements Wilde made during his lecture tour, but at the same time it should not be over emphasized. As we shall see, the views he expressed in America are generally consistent with statements he made later, in other contexts, such as his English journalism.

As Wilde travelled across America on his tour he left a trail of nationalist comments in his wake during newspaper interviews. On 10 February 1882, in Chicago, Wilde called his native country the mournful 'Niobe of Nations',[31] while Saint Patrick's Day found him in St Paul, Minnesota, where he made an impromptu speech at an Irish cultural event. He was introduced to the predominantly Irish audience as 'the son of one of Ireland's noblest daughters ... who did much to keep the fire of patriotism burning brightly'. Wilde presented himself as the inheritor of Speranza's views, commenting that with the arrival of the English in the

A racist American trade card from 1882, entitled 'National Aesthetics', depicting a stereotyped Irishman with aesthetic affectations. It reveals the extent to which Wilde was associated with Irish nationalism in the US.

twelfth century Ireland's pre-eminent European artistic and intellectual culture had been destroyed. Irish Art, he continued, 'had no existence for over 700 years. And he was glad it had not, for art could not flourish under a tyrant. Art was an expression of the liberty-loving, beauty-loving sentiment of the people. But the artistic sentiment was not dead in the people … . And when Ireland gains her independence, its schools of art and other educational branches will be revived and Ireland will regain the proud position she once held among the nations of Europe.'[32]

On 5 April, at Platt's Hall in San Francisco, Wilde lectured on 'The Irish Poets of the Nineteenth Century' to an audience which included many Irish-Americans. In the course of this lecture, Wilde offered tributes to Irish political figures such as Daniel O'Connell and John Mitchel, as well as to the poets of the Young Ireland movement. These bards of '48 had been, he said, prepared to 'die' for 'Liberty' and their verse had become, 'the primary basis of Irish politics, the keystone of Irish Liberty', the 'bulwark of patriotism'. Wilde praised his mother, and recited some of her revolutionary poems 'with much effect and feeling'. He peppered his talk with political statements with a strong contemporary resonance. He referred to the eighteenth-century 'legislative independence so unjustly robbed from us' by the English; he also commented: 'I do not know anything more wonderful, or characteristic of the Celtic genius than the quick artistic spirit in which we adapted ourselves to the English tongue. The Saxon took our lands and left them desolate. We took their language and added new beauty to it.' The press remarked on the strong nationalist cast of Wilde's comments, one paper describing him as a 'full-blown Land Leaguer.'[33]

Wilde had in fact recently discussed the Land League during an interview, published in the *St. Louis Globe Democrat* on 27 February 1882. We will dwell at length on the interview here because it constitutes Wilde's most detailed statement regarding Irish politics and because it is little known to Wilde scholarship.[34] The *Globe Democrat* reporter began by asking Wilde about his feelings with regard to the Land League.[35] 'As regards the general principle', Wilde replied, 'that the only basis of legislation should be the general welfare of the people, and that is the only test by which the right of any citizen to hold property or possess any privileges should be tested – I am entirely at one with the Land League. The land of Ireland ... is perfectly unfairly divided, and the peasantry ... have lived in the most impoverished way, in a state of life in which the only opening for them was to leave their country'.

Having lauded the general aims of the League, Wilde then qualified his praise. The League's No-Rent Manifesto, he said, was widely, and erroneously, taken to mean that the peasants and tenants should pay absolutely no rent to landlords – a position which 'I have no doubt that the most thoughtful amongst the Land League would not approve of.' Wilde was speaking as a property owner (he had inherited four houses in Bray on his father's death in 1876), and as the son of land-owners for whom reduced rents created acute financial difficulties.[36]

Wilde then dissected the recent 1881 Land Act, which had been introduced by Gladstone's Liberal Government, with the aim of enshrining in English Law the 'Three Fs' (fair rent, fixity of tenure and free sale of land) the Land League had campaigned for. 'The mistake', Wilde remarked apropos of the lack of compensation the Act gave to landlords, 'which I think the English government are making is in thinking they can permanently benefit one class in a community by permanently impoverishing the other. Up to this the gentry of Ireland have been rich and the peasants poor'. But the government 'have merely transferred the burden from the peasant to the educated classes' and thus 'have swept away a great deal of the best civilisation in Ireland. ... What I should wish to see', he concluded, 'would be the government purchasing the land of Ireland from the landlords at a fair rate.... A compulsory sale and a fair compensation clause seems to me to be the remedy.'

There was no essential contradiction between Wilde's support for the League and his advocacy of the rights of Anglo-Irish landlords; indeed, he offered a quintessentially Parnellite solution. Parnell advocated giving tenants and peasants a freehold in the land, with compensation to landlords. He may have seen this as the best deal on the table for his caste; in addition, he appears to have viewed it as a means of encouraging them to 'join the national ranks'.[37]

Parnell's opinions blended carefully selected elements of Land League radicalism and popular nationalist idealism, with political astuteness and Anglo-Irish social conservatism. Flexible and capacious, his views formed a cocktail that appealed strongly to the Wildes. In the 1880s, Speranza described Parnell as 'the man of destiny; he will strike off the fetters and free Ireland, and throne her as Queen among the nations.'[38] Her son Oscar was equally enthusiastic, publicly declaring himself 'strongly in sympathy with the Parnell movement' and privately praising Parnell's personality.[39] During his interview with the St Louis reporter, Wilde praised 'the most thoughtful amongst the Land League', and he was probably thinking of Parnell, among others. He may likewise have had Parnell in mind when he expatiated on the profound and positive influence of American Republican 'thought on Irish politics', which represented, he said, 'an entirely new departure in the history of Ireland'.[40] The *Globe Democrat* journalist then asked Wilde if he knew Parnell personally, and Wilde responded in the affirmative.[41] There seems little reason to question the veracity of his answer, which has escaped the notice of Wilde's critics and biographers.[42]

'Are you in favour of the total separation of Ireland from the United Kingdom?' the *Globe Democrat* reporter enquired. 'It is only a question', Wilde responded, 'of whether a country is able to assert its independence. At present, I think it would be unwise in Ireland to claim total separation, because I do not think she would be able to preserve it, and to attempt anything that one can not do is the only crime in politics. The first step to do should be a local Parliament, which I sincerely hope they will get, and it is an issue which my father was one of the first men in Ireland to advocate.'[43]

Wilde was echoing Parnell, who campaigned for 'at least the restitution of Grattan's (pre-Act of Union) parliament', which would have established an independent legislature but maintained some of Ireland's links with the British Empire. Yet Parnell introduced a note of optimism and ambivalence, when he looked to the longer-term future, famously arguing that, 'no man has the right to fix the boundary to the march of a nation'.[44] Wilde was striking the same note when he spoke of the 'local parliament' as the 'first step'.

As to the means by which Land Reform and Home Rule might be campaigned for, Wilde adopted a 'scientific' and pragmatic viewpoint, in the tradition of Machiavelli: 'It is very easy', Wilde told the journalist, 'to object to the means of a revolution, to lay one's finger on certain excesses; the only way to judge of an agitation is by the success. ... Politics is a practical science. An unsuccessful revolution is merely treason; a successful one is a great era in the history of a country.' Elaborating this point he offered the example of the French Revolution: no historical event, he pointed out, 'produced so much immediate suffering and immediate crime' yet none 'was ever productive of so much permanent good afterward.'[45]

Before the reporter took his leave, he asked one final question by way of summing up: 'Then I may put you down as a Home Ruler?' 'You may', Wilde replied 'emphatically'. The reporter accordingly gave the interview the emphatic title 'A Home Ruler. Oscar Wilde Has Some Well-Settled Opinions on the Irish Question'.

Wilde's early views on English political parties

WILDE'S VIEWS ON English party-politics were influenced by his opinions on Ireland. He seems to have favoured the English party most likely to implement the Irish constitutional and land reforms he advocated. At the beginning of 1880s both the Tories (led by Benjamin Disraeli until his death in 1881) and Gladstone's Liberals were hostile to Home Rule, and both used coercive measures to quell rural protest in Ireland.

The Tories had been in power from 1874–1880, and their record on Ireland inspired anger among nationalists. Speranza criticised Disraeli for lacking imagination, knowledge and initiative when it came to her country: 'No large, liberal measures', she wrote, 'are ever thought of as a remedy ... complaint is answered by a Coercion bill.' For this reason – and also because she saw some hope for Ireland in Gladstone's recent declaration that all peoples had the 'natural right of self-government' – she favoured the Liberals, who would win the 1880 general election.[46] As Wilde made clear during his discussion of the Liberal Land Act of 1881 with the St Louis journalist, some of the Irish policies of Gladstone's new government disappointed him. The Wildes would also have opposed the Liberal Coercion Act of 1881, which allowed imprisonment without trial in Ireland, and was used to incarcerate Parnell after he had attacked the 1881 Land Act in print. Wilde's disillusionment with Gladstone's Irish policies may inform some comments he made on English party politics during his American Lecture tour. He told one American journalist that Westminster politics held 'no interest' for him, the bickering between 'Liberal and Conservative', being, in his view, a sideshow to the only vital issue – the struggle between 'civilization and barbarism'.[47]

Yet events in Ireland soon made Wilde change his lofty tone. On 6 May 1882 Lord Frederick Cavendish, the newly appointed Chief Secretary to Ireland, and his Under-Secretary Thomas Burke, were stabbed to death in Dublin's Phoenix Park by the 'Invincibles', a splinter group of the Fenian Irish Republican Brotherhood. Informed of the news on 7 May by a New York journalist, Wilde was shocked and disgusted.[48] At the same time he urged that people 'not blame the whole Irish nation for the acts of a few men' and remarked on 'how much England is to blame ... she is morally reaping the fruit of seven centuries of injustice.' Looking to the immediate future Wilde commented, 'There must be trouble ahead. I presume martial law will be proclaimed and the Conservative party must come into power again, though I don't care to see it there.'[49]

At a moment of political crisis Wilde abjured his Olympian attitude to Westminster party politics, to declare a definite preference for the Liberals over the Tories. This is (to our knowledge) the earliest of Wilde's surviving English party-political declarations, and it is significant that it was inspired by events in Ireland. Of course, from Wilde's nationalist point of view, he was choosing the lesser evil – he expected further coercive measures to be introduced to Ireland, and merely hoped that a Liberal government would be less severe than a Tory one. In the event Gladstone extended the coercive measures already in place.

The Liberals would stay in office until June 1885, when Gladstone's government fell, after being defeated on the budget by a coalition of Conservatives and Irish MPs. The IPP was angry at Liberal plans to renew coercion. Lord Salisbury (Disraeli's successor as Conservative leader) led an interim Tory government until the November election, using the time to court Parnell. The Chief, as Parnell was known among his MPs and supporters, was eventually persuaded that the Tories offered the best deal for Ireland, and advised the Irish electorate in England to vote against Gladstone. Parnell's pragmatic attitude to the English parties (which he is said to have disliked equally) may help us understand the ambivalence (and indifference) an Irish Home Ruler such as Wilde had expressed about them during his lecture tour.

Yet Wilde apparently could not bring himself to obey his chief. Writing just before the election to his Oxford friend, the Conservative candidate George Curzon, Wilde indicated which way he would be casting his vote by describing himself as 'a Radical ...'.[50] The Radicals formed the most progressive faction of the Liberal Party, being vociferous advocates of social reform. Sir Charles Dilke, a personal acquaintance of Wilde's, was the Radical (Liberal) MP for Wilde's Chelsea constituency, and he had a strong aversion to coercion in Ireland.

At the 1885 election 335 Liberal MPs (including Dilke), 249 Conservative MPs, and 86 Irish MPs were returned. The Irish thus held the exact balance of parliamentary power. Parnell used the Irish votes to prop up a minority Tory government, but his rapprochement with Salisbury did not last long into the New Year. By that time the Home Rule proposals of the Earl of Carnarvon (the remarkably progressive Tory Lord Lieutenant for Ireland) had been rejected outright by the cabinet, and the Tories had decided to renew coercion. Even more importantly, Gladstone had, over the winter of 1885–1886, publicly declared himself a zealous convert to the Home Rule cause – the first time in recent history that an English party leader had advocated a degree of Irish autonomy. In consequence, Parnell now transferred his support to Gladstone, on the understanding that a Home

Rule bill would soon be introduced; and the 'Grand Old Man' (now in his late seventies) formed his third Liberal government. Soon after Gladstone introduced the First Home Rule Bill which, as we have seen, was defeated in July 1886. His government collapsed and was replaced, following a general election, by a coalition of Salisbury's Tories and the Liberal Unionists, who pursued a policy of severe coercion in Ireland.

Wilde's reaction to Tory coercion

WILDE'S REACTION TO Tory policy in Ireland is well known. In a series of book reviews, written over the next three years, mainly for the pro-Gladstone, pro-Home Rule *Pall Mall Gazette* (*PMG*), and later in the Liberal *Speaker*, Wilde fiercely condemned Balfour for his 'coercion and active misgovernment in Ireland'.[51] 'Mr. Balfour is very anxious', he wrote in one article, 'that Mr. William O'Brien should wear prison clothes, sleep on a plank bed, and be subjected to other indignities'.[52] Another review was dedicated to Wilfrid Blunt's *In Vinculis*, a volume of poems 'composed in the bleak cell of Galway prison', where the ardent Home Rule campaigner had been incarcerated by Balfour. According to Wilde, *In Vinculis* proved that while Balfour 'may enforce "plain living" by his prison regulations he cannot prevent "high thinking" or in any way limit or constrain the freedom of man's soul'. In other reviews Wilde made a point of criticising Tory poets and Unionists whenever he could. He mocked the anti-Home Ruler Swinburne for his 'strong affection for the Tory party', he was scathing about John Grant, the 'Laureate to the Primrose League' (a rank-and-file Tory organization) and a vociferous advocate of coercion, and he lambasted his old Classics tutor J.P. Mahaffy for his repressive Unionist views.[53]

Wilde also expressed his nationalist views through his editorship of *The Woman's World*. In late 1887 he was appointed editor by Thomas Wemyss Reid, the manager of Cassell, who published the magazine. Reid, a dyed-in-the-wool Gladstonian Liberal, Home Ruler and member of the Eighty Club, was aware of Wilde's politics.[54] He allowed Wilde, over the course of a two-year editorship, to publish a number of tendentious pieces on Irish topics, along with Lady Sandhurst's 'On Woman's Work in Politics', which was thinly-veiled propaganda for the Irish and Gladstonian Liberal causes.[55]

Around this time Wilde also began to introduce party-political references into his literary works. In particular he made a number of snide allusions to the Radical Liberal Unionists who, it seems, he could not forgive for leaving the Liberal Party and allying themselves with the Conservatives, in opposition to Home Rule. At the beginning of his short story 'Lord Arthur Savile's Crime', published in May 1887, Wilde describes a fashionable society reception to which 'violent Radicals' are now admitted, by virtue of their support for Salisbury's government. They chat away 'affably' with 'Gorgeous peeresses', and mix with 'Six [Tory] Cabinet Ministers ... in their stars and ribands'. This is the first of many Wildean jibes against the Radicals, his criticisms characteristically emphasising their hypocrisy.[56]

In addition, Wilde made his feelings clear on both coercion and the 'Irish question' generally, by attending a nationalist meeting of the Southwark Irish Literary Club on 21 September 1887. The club was an offshoot of the Land League, and a centre of Young Ireland type propagandism, which aimed to spread knowledge of Irish history and literature in the English capital with a nationalist political end in mind.[57] At the meeting a lecture on 'the poets of '48', was delivered by IPP MP Justin McCarthy (one of several IPP MPs involved in the club). During his talk McCarthy declared that the Young Irelanders had 'laid the way for everything that had happened since ... . Having seen in their dreams that it was possible to make Ireland hold her own again', Irish MPs had then 'worked till they had made it a genuine reality.' And now, he said, because of their joint efforts, 'a National Government for Ireland' was all but inevitable, even Balfour admitting 'in his heart and to his friends that the question was settled'. After McCarthy sat down, the 'exquisitely dressed' Wilde rose to make a 'complimentary speech' about the lecture, to 'loud cheers'. In the course of this he remarked that he 'had ever held as sacred the names of those distinguished countrymen of his mentioned by the lecturer [i.e. the poets of '48]'.[58] He also praised the work of the club and promised to present it with a copy of *Ancient Legends* – the recently-published volume of Irish legends, superstitions and charms edited by his mother (whose poetry McCarthy had praised in the course of his lecture). This was a fitting gesture as the legends in Speranza's anthology are infused with nationalist sentiments.[59]

The Parnell Commission

WE ARE NOW in a position to understand why Wilde decided to join the Eighty Club in 1887. It is comprehensible in the light of his long-standing nationalism, his often expressed Parnellite Home Rule views, and his increasing preference for the Liberals over the Tories in the course of the 1880s. In addition it can be seen as a further expression of his hostility towards Tory coercion in Ireland.

Despite the failure of Gladstone's 1886 Home Rule Bill and the subsequent collapse of the Liberal government and the Tory election victory, 1887 was a time of optimism among Home Rulers. Wilde's decision to join the club may reflect this. Justin McCarthy's conviction that the constitutional question was settled was echoed by other Irish MPs. Nationalist confidence was founded upon the solid alliance between the IPP and the Liberals, as well as on the experience, skill and enormous popular appeal of both Gladstone and Parnell. With such advantages it is unsurprising that the end of direct English rule in Ireland, and the achievement of some sort of independent government and an equitable solution to the land question, seemed all but inevitable. Many Gladstonian Liberals were confident they could convert the British electorate to the Home Rule cause, and so win the next general election. Even if they failed to do so, IPP and Gladstonian Liberal Home Rulers would still constitute a significant presence at Westminster, thus ensuring the 'Irish question' would continue to be asked at virtually every Westminster session. In these circumstances it would have to be answered sooner or later.

Home Rule is the leitmotif of Wilde's eight-year Eighty Club career (1887–1895), as the following narrative will demonstrate. Our account will also reveal how Wilde's club activities dovetail with his other nationalist undertakings during the same period.

On 13 December 1887 Wilde attended what appears to have been his first Eighty Club event – a dinner at Willis's Rooms, King Street, London. Club dinners were attended by members, along with guests. At the head table sat the main speaker, the chairman for the evening, and the proposer and the seconder of the votes of thanks. After dinner, further guests (including some women) would come in to listen to the speeches.

The format of the speeches at club dinners was always the same – an introduction from the chair, followed by the main speaker, and then an epilogue, comprised of a proposal and seconding of the vote of thanks, with a reply from the main speaker. On this occasion the chairman was William Robson (a Vice President of the club and former Liberal MP). He opened the meeting by alluding to the sad defection of the Liberal Unionists from the party, before launching into a diatribe against Tory coercion in Ireland. His comments were received with cheers from the company. Robson then introduced the main speaker, Lord Granville, a former Foreign Secretary who had recently retired from public life and one of the few Whig grandees who supported Home Rule. Granville took up Robson's theme of the Tories' mismanagement of Ireland, accusing the Conservatives of trying to 'suspend the Irish question', the only answer to which was Home Rule. His speech was met with vociferous approval from the audience, which likewise enthusiastically endorsed the proposal and seconding of the vote of thanks.[60]

Some weeks after the dinner Wilde received his first copy of the club's annual publication, *The Eighty Club*, sent to members early each year. The booklet contained a statement of the club's objects and rules, a list of members and those who served on the committee, a summary of the previous year's activities, and verbatim reports of the speeches (such as Granville's) given at dinners over the course of the year. Wilde appears to have kept these annual club publications in his library – a club booklet belonging to him has survived, and seems to have been part of his book collection.[61]

In May 1888 Wilde made plans to attend another club dinner. Writing to his friend, the Cambridge don and author Oscar Browning, he asked, 'Are you a member of the Eighty Club? If not will you dine with me on Tuesday May 8th at Willis's Rooms – 7.30 – at the dinner where Parnell is to speak. It will be an extremely interesting occasion.'[62] Wilde's name is not included in official lists of those present so perhaps he was unable to attend, or failed to secure a place at dinner. Yet official club lists are not always complete, so Wilde may have been among the diners (it seems unlikely that Wilde would have invited a guest to the dinner, had he not secured a place for himself).[63]

At the dinner, the chairman for the evening, Richard Haldane (MP for Haddingtonshire and Eighty Club Vice President) introduced Parnell as 'the leader of the other wing of the allied army'. The allies would, Haldane averred, soon establish an Irish parliament, and settle the land question, bringing justice to all classes – landlord as well as tenant. Haldane's preamble over, Parnell received a standing ovation that lasted several minutes.[64] The Chief remained impassive as he waited for the applause to cease. When it died down he calmly affirmed his commitment to the alliance with Liberals, and expressed a measured and qualified support for the 'Plan of Campaign'. He ended by prophesying the ultimate victory of Home Rule, while warning that 'great trouble' lay ahead for the remainder of the Tory government, if it persisted with its repressive policies.[65]

Wilde may have wanted to attend the 8 May meeting in part to express solidarity with Parnell. According to the *PMG*, the Chief was, in the very same week, being vilified in *The Times* as an inciter of violence, with whom it would be iniquitous to 'sit down to table'.[66] Ever since the previous spring the pro-Tory newspaper had been publishing articles under the title 'Parnellism and Crime', in which it claimed that the Irish leader approved of terrorist violence and, in particular, of the Phoenix Park murders of 1882. To support this assertion the paper reproduced the facsimile of a letter apparently written by Parnell, in which he remarked that 'Burke got no more than his just deserts', and regretted that he was forced to denounce the murders in public for political reasons. Parnell had condemned the letter in the Commons as a 'villainous and bare-faced forgery', but *The Times* continued its onslaught.[67]

The Times publicly challenged Parnell to bring a libel action against them, but he declined to do so. However, the former Irish MP Frank O'Donnell did take the paper to court on the grounds (false as it turned out) that it had implicated him along with Parnell. When the O'Donnell case was heard at the beginning of July 1888, Wilde attended some of the sessions, sitting 'not far removed from the end of the jury-box ... on the platform in line with the judgment seat, in most artistic pose'.[68] During the trial the counsel for the defence repeated *The Times*' accusations against Parnell, adding fresh evidence of incitement to murder – it was as though Parnell, and by extension the Home Rule cause, were on trial.

Parnell responded to the new charges with another denial in the Commons; in addition he demanded that a Select Committee of the House be set up to investigate the letters quoted by *The Times*. The Tory government refused, choosing instead to appoint a Special Commission under three die-hard Unionist judges, to enquire not only into the letters but also into the myriad other charges *The Times* had brought against Irish leaders, thus increasing the chances that some mud might stick. The Commission began its work in September, but would not examine the letters until February 1889.

In the winter of 1888–1889 Wilde made a number of private and public declarations of his patriotism. In November, he wrote to Gladstone to express 'the deep admiration that I along with my countrymen feel for the one English statesman who has understood us, who has sympathised with us, whom we claim now as our leader, and who, we know well, will lead us to the grandest and justest political victory of this age.'[69] A few weeks later Wilde described himself, to the managing editor of the new Tory (and anti-Home Rule) paper *The Scots Observer: An Imperial Review*, as 'a most recalcitrant patriot'.[70] At the beginning of 1889 Wilde offered to help with the 'formation of a committee of National Protest' against 'the systematic injustice and inhumanity of Mr Balfour's rule in Ireland'; he added his name to a list of prominent people who condemned the 'grave, moral, and national crime' of coercion; their protest was published in the Irish *Freeman's Journal and Daily Commercial Advertiser*.[71] Such gestures did not, it seems, go unnoticed; Wilde was spoken of in the press as an ardent Home Ruler, one newspaper describing him as 'the cheeriest and most pronounced of Nationalists ... even if Protestant and land-lord bred' and suffering in pocket through his tenants' non-payment of rent.[72]

All nationalist eyes turned to the Parnell Commission in February 1889. Wilde attended several of its sessions during that month and was on intimate terms with Parnell's solicitor George Lewis (Lewis, a key participant in the Commission, was Wilde's solicitor; in March 1889 he would become a member of the Eighty Club). Wilde's keen interest in the Commission is also evidenced by his acquisition of a published account of its proceedings.[73] The artist S.P. Hall made a sketch of Wilde sitting in

Sketch of the Parnell Commission by Sydney Prior Hall. Parnell is the rightmost figure on the front row; beside him is Michael Davitt. Sir George Lewis is the rightmost figure on the second row.

the courtroom during one session in early February – dressed in an overcoat, with a cigarette in his gloved hand, his head is turned to the right as he gazes intently on (see front cover).[74]

On 20 February Wilde arrived at the court to find it full, and was forced to wait in the corridor until a place in the public area became free. He appears to have eventually found a place next to Wemyss Reid.[75] Demand for seats was high because a breakthrough was anticipated from Parnell's counsel, Sir Charles Russell (Irishman, Liberal MP for Hackney South and a Vice President of the Eighty Club). Russell had cast doubt on the authenticity of the 'Parnell' letters, successfully demonstrating that *The Times* had printed them without enquiring too closely into their provenance, out of eagerness to discredit the Irish leader and

Gladstone. All the evidence Russell had cited suggested the letters were forgeries, and pointed to the Irish journalist Richard Pigott as the forger. It was on 20 February that Pigott entered the witness-box for the first time. Russell began a devastating cross-examination, which would continue over the next few days and which Wilde's brother Willie enthusiastically described, in *The Daily Chronicle* of 23 February, as a 'masterpiece of humorous severity'. Under the pressure of Russell's onslaught Pigott first faltered and then collapsed, all but admitting his guilt (soon after the forger fled to Madrid, where he committed suicide). Parnell and the Home Rule cause were vindicated.

Appropriately, Wilde celebrated Parnell's exoneration by attending an Eighty Club dinner at Willis's Rooms on 8 March 1889, organized partly in honour of the Chief. At the head table sat the chairman Frank Lockwood (the Liberal MP for York) and the main speaker, Lord Spencer, a Whig grandee and former Liberal Lord Lieutenant of Ireland. Next to them sat Rosebery, Russell and Haldane. 'All shades of fighting Liberalism' were represented on other tables – pro-Gladstone journalists chatted away with prominent Liberal MPs, while Wilde 'with a big bunch of violets' in his buttonhole, provided, as it were, the 'link between journalism and art'. Not far from Wilde sat the Irish MPs T.P. O'Connor and Justin McCarthy, both acquaintances of his.

Parnell was running late, but out of a feeling of awe no one touched their food until he arrived. When he finally entered the room he 'unostentatiously' walked over to the head table, 'accompanied the while by deafening cheers'. Seeing Lord Spencer, Parnell extended his hand – a historic handshake given the fact that Spencer had been Ireland's Lord Lieutenant at the time of the Phoenix Park murders, and responsible for implementing the coercion that followed in their wake.

Dinner over, Lockwood introduced Spencer, who launched into a eulogy of Parnell and a fierce denunciation of the Tory government, for seeming to have assisted *The Times* in an attack of surpassing 'vehemence and bitterness and wickedness'. On finishing he sat down to cheers. The audience then began to demand an impromptu speech from Parnell – something that went against both club etiquette and the Chief's inclination. Such was the clamour however that finally Parnell rose to his feet. As he did so the entire audience rose with him and waved their napkins over their heads. In the commotion the heat in the room became unbearable.

Terse, deadpan and dignified, Parnell made no reference whatsoever to the recent Commission; he did, however, take a sideswipe at 'mushrooms like Balfour', which the company enjoyed immensely. He concluded optimistically, looking forward to a time 'in the very near future' when his country would secure recognition of its claims and interests. The Chief then sat down to loud cheers. Rosebery wound up proceedings by proposing a vote of thanks to the speakers. Wilde's acquaintance, Augustine Birrell (an essayist who was soon to enter parliament) seconded the vote.[76]

An active Eighty Clubber

THE NEXT MEETING of the Eighty Club Wilde attended was held at the Westminster Palace Hotel on 10 April 1889. For this conversazione, John Morley (the popular Liberal MP, devoted Gladstone disciple, and honourable Eighty Club member) was advertised as the main speaker. Wilde was chosen to propose a vote of thanks after his speech. The committee's decision to ask Wilde to speak (and moreover to speak after such an important figure within the party) indicates his growing prominence within the club; indeed, he was one of only three members invited to propose a vote of thanks in 1889, and previous proposers included Rosebery and Asquith.[77] The committee presumably viewed the speech as part of the political work Wilde had pledged to perform on joining the Eighty.

Unfortunately no detailed record of Wilde's proposal appears to have survived. The club published no official account of the conversazione, and the newspaper reports of it are disappointingly brief. No manuscript of the talk has survived – if indeed one ever existed (which seems unlikely, Wilde being so seasoned a speaker). Nevertheless, using newspaper reports, along with a variety of other sources, it is possible to reconstruct certain aspects of the evening.

The meeting took place in the 'long and leathery' elongated soirée room of the hotel. It was attended by 510 members and guests (an exceptionally large number), who sat in armchairs or stood along the sides of the room, propping themselves up between the paintings.[78] Edward Marjoribanks (Liberal MP for Berwickshire) was in the chair for the occasion. He opened the proceedings by explaining that John Morley had regrettably been unable to attend due to a severe cold, and that Henry Fowler (Liberal MP for Wolverhampton East) would be standing in for him. He then discussed the recent progress made by the Liberal party in 'inducing many thoughtful men to reconsider their views on the Irish question', and even prompting their Tory opponents to doubt their draconian policy. In particular, Marjoribanks highlighted the influence of Sir Charles Russell's 'splendid vindication of the Irish nation' at the Parnell Commission, which had analysed historic, and more recent, misgovernment and misrule in the country.

Having been introduced by Marjoribanks, Henry Fowler surveyed the political scene. He predicted a great future for the Party, and criticised the Conservatives, especially for employing 'forged evidence' and 'the aid of perjurers' in its attacks on Parnell; like Marjoribanks he praised Sir Charles Russell's Commission speech. He ended by outlining the Home Rule legislation Gladstone would introduce in parliament when they regained power, which would enshrine the principles that 'the Irish people should manage their own affairs', and that 'the unity of the Empire should be preserved'.[79]

When Fowler sat down Wilde rose to propose a vote of thanks. The task of the proposer was to praise the speaker, and to offer a personal perspective on the issues covered in the speaker's talk, garnishing his comments with anecdotes. The length of the proposal could be between five and ten minutes, and the tone and style depended on the occasion and on the proposer's personal taste. Proposals in fact came in all colours – some were formal, some were fiery, others were fun.

If Wilde followed club protocol, he would have echoed Fowler in his choice of subjects. This means that he would have discussed the Tory attacks on Parnell, the Commission and Home Rule. In doing Wilde may have rehearsed some of the 'well-settled opinions' on Irish issues he had voiced during his American lecture tour; however, a man with Wilde's telepathic sensitivity to his listeners would probably not have spoken quite as emphatically as he had done in the United States.

Wilde would surely have felt comfortable in criticising Tory policy in Ireland and the party's attacks on the Irish leaders. The Conservative government's Irish policy, and English misgovernment of Ireland generally, were subjects at the forefront of his mind at this time. Only three days after the Eighty's conversazione the *PMG* published Wilde's review of J.A. Froude's Irish historical novel, *Two Chiefs of Dunboy*, printing it above his initials (uniquely for one of Wilde's *PMG* reviews). 'Blue Books are generally dull reading', the review begins, 'but Blue Books on Ireland have always been interesting. They form the record of one of the great tragedies of modern Europe. In them England has written down her indictment against herself, and has given to the world the history of her shame.' Later on in the article Wilde suggests that 'law and order' English government in Ireland generally means 'the enforcement of unjust legislation' and 'the suppression of every fine national aspiration'; he also wonders whether Froude's book, which promotes 'the idea of solving the Irish question by doing away with the Irish people', was written 'to help the Tory Government to solve the Irish question.' Wilde also mentions that Ireland's 'first practical leader is an Irish-American' – an enthusiastic and unmistakable reference to Parnell, whose mother was American.[80]

A few months later Wilde was asked to reprise his oratorical turn at a November meeting of the Cambridge University Liberal Club (CULC), where he appears to have represented the Eighty. The CULC, which had been founded in 1886, was the first ever English university political society. Its aim was to disseminate

> 1895.
>
> # THE "EIGHTY" CLUB.
>
> ## CONTENTS.
>
> | | |
> |---|---|
> | COMMITTEE ... ... | 2 |
> | OBJECTS ... ... | 3—4 |
> | RULES ... ... | 5—8 |
> | REPORT FOR 1894 ... ... | 9—17 |
> | LIST OF MEMBERS ... ... | 17—34 |
>
> *Speeches and Pamphlets published during the year:*
>
> "The House of Lords," by T. A. Spalding.
>
> "Labour Questions," by B. Pickard, M.P.
>
> "Party Prospects," by Sir F. Lockwood, Q.C., M.P.
>
> "The Lords, Labour and Liberalism," by Right Hon. Lord Tweedmouth.
>
> "The House of Lords," by Sir F. Lockwood, Q.C., M.P.
>
> "Liberal Programme and the House of Lords," by Right Hon. Earl of Kimberley, K.G.
>
> "London Government," by Sidney Webb.

An Eighty Club pamphlet from 1895 summarising the club's activities since 1879. Wilde's vote of thanks at the 10 April 1889 meeting is mentioned; Wilde is also listed among the current members of the club. The last year of his membership was 1895.

'Liberal Principles among the undergraduate members of the University [and] with this view the club affiliated itself with the Eighty Club, members of which ... from time to time come down to Cambridge, and by means of addresses, stimulate the efforts of the younger generation of University men in the good old cause'.[81]

The CULC meetings at which Eighty Club members spoke were sometimes formal affairs involving long political speeches. In addition the club hosted regular informal smoking concerts. Many of these gatherings were organized and presided over by the King's College don Oscar Browning, a prominent Eighty Club member and the treasurer of the CULC, who dominated the university club's early years. Wilde had known Browning since at least 1879, and it seems likely it was Browning who asked Wilde to speak at a CULC event. We know that Browning had invited Wilde up to Cambridge in the summer of 1889, and that Wilde had made plans for the trip; however, at the last minute, Wilde had been forced to put off his visit to a future date.[82] His presence at the November meeting may represent the fulfilment of his promise.

The meeting at which Wilde almost certainly spoke was held on Wednesday the 20th, at Gonville and Caius College. Very few details concerning it have come down to us, as it does not seem to have been covered in the local press. The lack of coverage suggests it was an informal meeting, perhaps along the lines of one of Browning's smoking concerts. Lord Monkswell (Wilde's fellow Chelsea resident and Eighty Club member) also spoke at the event.[83] As 'access was tightly controlled, with tickets needing the signature of one of the two club secretaries', it is likely that the venue was small and that only a portion of the club's 200 members attended. Male undergraduate members of the CULC would have comprised the bulk of the audience; there would also have been some female guests and dons.[84]

We do not know the content of Wilde's CULC speech, as no record of his words appears to have survived. However both his speech and Monkswell's would have been political in scope, though they may conceivably have touched on other topics. Typically Eighty Club speakers took up a burning Liberal issue of the day and, in the late 1880s and early 1890s, the issue was, more often than not, Home Rule. Asquith and Sir Robert Reid made it the subject of their CULC addresses; Irish MPs such as Justin McCarthy and William O'Brien gave talks on Ireland to the club. It seems likely then that Wilde would have at least mentioned Home Rule in the course of his address, but until a report of the evening is unearthed, we cannot be certain.

Through his regular attendance at the Eighty Club, and through his speeches, Wilde had, by the end of 1889, established himself as a prominent and active club member. From the social invitations he received in the course of that year it is clear that he was, in addition, accepted by the Liberal political élite (and here, his membership of the Eighty may have served him as a passport). In May Wilde and his wife Constance were invited to 'the political dinner of the year', given by Sir Charles Russell, at which the Gladstones, Parnell, the Blunts, Lady Sandhurst and Justin McCarthy were present.[85] Soon after the Wildes attended the Eighty Club's celebration of the Gladstones' golden wedding anniversary.[86] The Gladstones also signed Constance's autograph book, apparently at another society party.[87] Around this time Liberal MPs such as Asquith and William Grenfell welcomed Wilde to their homes, where the legendary storyteller would enchant the other guests with his marvellous tales. At the end of the year Wilde's position within the Liberal intelligentsia was acknowledged, and strengthened further, when he was invited by Wemyss Reid to a dinner for contributors to the new Liberal journal, *The Speaker*. Held at the Reform Club, the dinner was attended by twenty five people, among whom were three

Liberal MPs, a prominent Parnellite, and ten members of the Eighty Club. Soon afterwards Wilde wrote two long reviews for the publication.[88]

Over the same period Wilde socialized regularly with members of Parnell's IPP. At Liberal parties he met men such as Barry O'Brien, Justin McCarthy, and James Carew (Parnell's confidant).[89] Wilde saw much of T.P. O'Connor and his wife in the late 1880s. 'Mrs T.P.' recalled being introduced to Wilde by Justin McCarthy's daughter at one of Lady St Helier's London salons.[90] She also remembered seeing Wilde and his wife at an 1888 reception of O'Connor's newspaper, *The Star*, at which Gladstone and Sir Charles Russell were present.[91] In 1889 Mrs T.P. invited Wilde to her celebrated weekly parties 'where', according to an American newspaper, 'you will meet, very often, such persons as Mr Gladstone, Mr Parnell, Lord Rosebery, the McCarthys, père and fils ... Oscar Wilde'.[92] Around this time O'Connor inscribed Constance's autograph book: 'There is something almost bewildering in the thought that this generation of Irishmen is about to see the close of a struggle that has gone through seven centuries'.[93]

By the beginning of the nineties, Wilde readily identified himself as (and was also well known as) both a Home Ruler and a Gladstonian Liberal. This can be gauged from a letter he wrote to the Tory MP for Chelsea, Charles Whitmore, in January 1890, to recommend his personal doctor to the post of Chelsea's Divisional Surgeon of the Police. 'Since my marriage he has been my family doctor', Wilde wrote, 'and though you converted him to Unionism at the last election, we have not changed him! So I am not helping my party in this matter.'[94]

Parnell's downfall

WILDE ATTENDED A 'semi-political party' given by his friend, the Liberal MP Cyril Flower, for Eighty Club members on 14 May 1890. The *World* waspishly reported that Wilde vied with Oscar Browning for the attention of the guests, by 'retailing well-worn anecdotes'.[95] The following month he was present at a club conversazione attended by forty or so members.[96] The mood of some of the guests at these parties may have been subdued as, once again, a cloud had risen in the west.

At the end of 1889 Parnell had been cited as co-respondent in a divorce case filed by Captain O'Shea, whose wife Katherine had been the Irish leader's partner for around a decade. Parnell declined to contest the case, as he wanted Katherine to obtain a divorce and so be free to marry him. When the court case of November 1890 made public the intimate details of Parnell's private life, *The Times* gleefully stoked up the scandal.

As a result of the scandal the so-called Nonconformist conscience Liberals, who comprised a large portion of Liberal voters and party members, threatened to withdraw their support if Gladstone failed to cut ties with the wicked Irish adulterer. On 25 November 1890 the Liberal leader delivered an ultimatum to Parnell – if he did not resign as leader of the IPP, the Liberals would break the alliance. Utterly indifferent to what the English public thought of him, Parnell refused to stand down. His MPs now had to choose between supporting their leader and maintaining links with the Liberals. In the end the IPP split into Parnellite and anti-Parnellite factions (the latter led by Justin McCarthy), with Parnell's supporters forming only the rump.

Continually attacked by prominent Irish political and religious figures over the ensuing months, and visibly weakened by a serious kidney disease, Parnell was a diminished political force. He had also burned his bridges so far as Liberals were concerned, by publicly branding Gladstone a traitor to Ireland, and delivering speeches laced with Anglophobia.[97] For all Home Rulers, and especially for people who revered Parnell, the winter months of 1890–1891 were a trying time.

Parnell's sudden fall, first from grace and then from power, may have contributed to the angry mood in which Wilde picked up his pen in the early months of 1891. He added several chapters to his novella *The Picture of Dorian Gray*, which had been published in *Lippincott's Magazine* in June 1890 to some outraged and outrageous reviews.[98] In the new chapters, penned for the story's publication in book format as a novel, Wilde characterized England as 'the native land of the hypocrite', and the English as a race that 'balance stupidity with wealth, and vice by hypocrisy'.[99]

Over the winter Wilde also completed his political essay 'The Soul of Man under Socialism', which was published in the February 1891 issue of the Liberal periodical *The Fortnightly Review*. Attacking the 'stupidity, and hypocrisy, and Philistinism' that pervade English culture, Wilde rails against English public opinion which, he says, exercises a 'tyranny' over art, politics and 'people's private lives' through the press. Wilde singles out 'the serious ... journalists, who solemnly, as they are doing at present, will drag before the eyes of the public some incident in the private life of a great statesman, of a man who is a leader of political thought as he is a creator of political force, and invite the public to ... exercise authority in the matter ... to dictate to the man upon all other points, to dictate to his party, to dictate to his country... . The private lives of men and women should not be told to the public. The public have nothing to do with them at all. In France they manage these things better. There they do not allow the details of the trials that take place in the divorce courts to be published for the amusement or criticism of the public. All that the public are allowed to know is that the divorce has taken place and was granted on petition of one or other or both of the married parties concerned.'[100] Printed in the *Fortnightly*, in early 1891, these words could only be read as an indictment of Parnell's oppressors.[101] Yet surprisingly several editors of Wilde's essay seem reluctant to read the passage as an obvious allusion to Parnell, suggesting Wilde may have had a number of figures in mind, including former Radical MP Charles Dilke.[102]

Wilde attended two Eighty Club at homes in 1891, and one on 15 June 1892. This seems to be his last ever appearance at a club meeting. The account books of the club reveal that he dutifully renewed his membership in 1893 and 1894, yet these years of his membership are otherwise a blank.[103] Similarly, he does not appear to have attended any Liberal social events after the spring of 1891, so 1891–1892 effectively marks the end of his active involvement with club and party.

There may have been personal and professional reasons for his waning interest. The curtain was about to go up on Wilde's intense and time-consuming affair with Lord Alfred Douglas. Moreover, with the production of Wilde's society comedies (the first of which he started penning in early 1891) he achieved fame and fortune and these gods (like love) made enormous demands on his time. Yet political factors were probably more important. Wilde may have resented the Liberal Party's role in Parnell's downfall and felt alienated from the Eighty Club because of it. The club had naturally rallied round its President, Gladstone, in the wake of the Parnell scandal and subsequent political crisis.

George Trevelyan, for example, remarked at a club meeting on 2 December 1890 that the 'Irish cause has been and is in troubled waters; but it is in troubled waters and under a dark sky that we most require that the pilot should steer a straight course; and our pilot has been equal to the supreme occasion.'[104] Members of the club may even have felt some embarrassment at their former championing of Parnell, as Tories and Liberal Unionists publically ridiculed the Eighty for having made 'much of him as their guest'.[105] It may not be entirely coincidental that the IPP member (and Wilde's acquaintance) Justin Huntley McCarthy lost interest in the club around the same time as Wilde. The Eighty's account books reveal that he resigned in late 1891 or early 1892, having joined the club, like Wilde, in 1887.

Whatever Wilde's view on the Liberal Party's handling of the crisis, and regardless of whether he supported the Parnell or Justin McCarthy faction of the IPP (though it is, in truth, hard to imagine him turning against his hero), he must have known that, without a charismatic and experienced leader at the head of a united Irish party, the chances of a Home Rule Bill passing through parliament were virtually non-existent. Moreover, the Liberal–IPP alliance would have seemed far less robust than it had done in 1887, with suspicion and resentment on both sides decreasing further the chances of achieving Irish autonomy at Westminster. The cooling of Wilde's ardour for Gladstonian Liberalism, and the anti-English anger that sears the pages of the 'Soul of Man' and *Dorian Gray*, can be seen more clearly against this dark background.[106]

A disillusioned Home Ruler; still a recalcitrant patriot

ON 6 OCTOBER 1891 Parnell died of a heart attack. 'Poor Parnell's death' wrote Constance Wilde to a friend, 'is the best solution of a difficulty, and ... things will now right themselves'.[107] The uncrowned king was dead, Constance seems to have been suggesting, yet there was a chance that the dissension among the Irish MPs might die with him – and if the party came together then the Home Rule cause might be resurrected. In the event, the Irish MPs did not unite, but they were at least one, in the lead up to the general election of July 1892, in pledging their support to the Liberals, who promised to introduce another Home Rule Bill if elected. If he voted at the election, Wilde would have undoubtedly voted for Gladstone's party once again.

Although Wilde appears to have no longer been a practicing Gladstonian Liberal he was no less of a 'recalcitrant patriot'. 'French by sympathy', he described himself in the winter of 1891–1892, 'I am Irish by race, and the English have condemned me to speak the language of Shakespeare';[108] 'I am not English', he told a journalist in June 1892, 'I'm Irish – which is quite another thing'.[109] Such statements produced political vibrations which the press seem to have picked up. A month later *Punch* printed a caricature of the nationalist author under the title 'A Wilde Idea, or, more Injustice to Ireland', a comment on the banning of Wilde's French language play *Salomé*, and Wilde's subsequent threat to apply for French citizenship.[110] Wilde also

'A Wilde Idea', J. Bernard Partridge's caricature for *Punch* (9 July 1892, p. 1) of Wilde in the uniform of a French conscript, which mocks his threat to apply for French citizenship.

affirmed his nationalism at this time by becoming one of the original members of the Irish Literary Society, which grew out of the Southwark Literary Society, and which played an important role in the Celtic Revival.[111]

At the election the Liberal–Irish coalition secured 45 seats more than the Tory–Liberal Unionist alliance. While this enabled Gladstone to form his fourth government, passing a Home Rule Bill with such a slender majority would be extremely difficult – for the Tory-dominated Lords to be coerced into approving a bill, the Commons majority would have to be so overwhelming as to carry with it the threat of a constitutional crisis. (The underwhelming election result may incidentally be another reason for Wilde's waning interest in party politics). Gladstone was undaunted however and introduced his Second Home Rule Bill to the Commons in the spring of 1893. It was fiercely debated over the summer.

Wilde was, at this time, renting a house in Goring-on-Thames in order to write his third social comedy, *An Ideal Husband*.[112] During his stay by the Thames he intervened in an argument over Home Rule which took place between an English acquaintance of his and his own eight-year-old son, Cyril. On hearing Wilde's acquaintance make a 'slighting remark about Home Rule', Cyril 'flushed with anger, and violently demanded whether [he] was not a Home Ruler'. At this point, Wilde interrupted with the comment 'My own idea is that Ireland should rule England'.[113]

At the beginning of September, the Second Home Rule Bill passed its third Commons reading, but was then immediately rejected by 378 votes in the Lords. Gladstone retired from politics in March 1894, to be replaced as Prime Minister by Rosebery, who had no intention of introducing another Irish Bill (indeed he would eventually renounce the Home Rule cause). The parliamentary movement for Irish independence was defeated, and would not be fully revived until the early twentieth century.

Wilde would make one further public statement regarding English party-politics, in his dramatic masterpiece *The Importance of Being Earnest*, written in the summer of 1894. When interviewing Jack Worthing as a candidate for her daughter's hand, the arch Tory Lady Bracknell, asks, 'What are your politics?' Jack replies candidly, 'Well, I am afraid I really have none. I am a Liberal Unionist'. To this Lady Bracknell responds, 'Oh, they count as Tories. They dine with us. Or come in the evening, at any rate.' Wilde thus mocks the emptiness, intellectual poverty and opportunism of the Liberal Unionists, while hinting at the low esteem in which their partners, the Tories, really hold them.[114]

Wilde's downfall and the Eighty Club

THERE IS AN obvious, and fearful, symmetry between Wilde's downfall in 1895, and Parnell's four years previously. Both were the consequence of private, sexual behaviour, but both had an Irish political dimension.[115] It may not be complete coincidence, for example, that Edward Carson QC, Balfour's former henchman, and now Unionist MP for Trinity College Dublin, cross-examined Wilde in court with such relish during the Queensberry libel trial. Nor can it be entirely happenstance that sections of the Tory press condemned, before he was tried, the nationalist sworn in as 'Oscar Fingal O'Fflahertie Wills Wilde', then gloated when he was eventually sentenced. There may be some truth then in Frank Harris' remark that Wilde had about as much chance of a fair trial at the Old Bailey as an Invincible.[116]

Yet Wilde's downfall is not simply another example of Tory coercion against an Irishman. In fact Wilde's prosecution was a thoroughly Liberal affair, being engineered and expedited primarily by his friends from the Eighty Club. Party grandees and luminaries who had embraced Wilde as one of their own now turned against him. The betrayals began right from the start. In late February 1895, when Wilde had charged the Marquess of Queensberry with libel for publicly referring to him as a 'posing Somdomite [sic]', the Marquess asked Sir George Lewis (Wilde's friend and fellow Eighty Club member) to act as his solicitor. Lewis at first agreed though he later withdrew from the case. It was then taken up by Charles Russell Junior, another Eighty Club member, who selected Carson as his defence barrister, on the recommendation of his father Sir Charles Russell, now Lord Chief Justice. (As we have seen, Wilde knew both Charles Russells – Sir Charles had invited Wilde to dinner in 1889, and Russell Junior had seconded Wilde's proposal of thanks at the club's conversazione the same year).

Immediately after the collapse of the Queensberry libel case, Charles Russell Junior contacted the Director of Public Prosecutions regarding Wilde's possible arrest. The Public Prosecutor then spoke with Sir Robert Reid (the Attorney-General), Frank Lockwood (the Solicitor-General) and Asquith (the Home Secretary) all of whom were Vice Presidents of the Eighty Club. Acquaintanceship and political kinship were put aside, however, as they decided to apply for an arrest warrant straightaway, though they were not legally bound to do so (Wilde's acquaintance, Lord Henry Somerset, had tactfully been given ample time to leave the country in similar circumstances). Wilde was charged with having committed gross indecency.

The jury failed to arrive at a verdict and this gave Lockwood a second chance to help Wilde. At that point, with Wilde publicly disgraced, and socially and professionally ruined, his persecution might have been dropped. Lockwood, however, not only decided that a re-trial should take place, but also put himself forward as counsel for the prosecution. At the trial he did his utmost to achieve a conviction, delivering an 'appalling denunciation' which 'sickened with horror' the man in the dock.[117] Lockwood's efforts proved successful as Wilde received a two-year sentence with hard labour.

Why was Wilde arrested so quickly, and why was he put on trial a second time? There is a strong suspicion of a Liberal conspiracy, with some commentators suggesting that Queensberry made a deal with the government. In exchange for Wilde's head,

Queensberry (or so the theory goes) offered the cabinet his silence on a potentially damaging matter – the love affair between the Prime Minister Rosebery and his son Drumlanrig, who had died by accident or suicide in October 1894.[118] When the Irish MP Tim Healy urged Lockwood not to try Wilde a second time the Solicitor-General replied, 'I wouldn't but for the abominable rumours against ******'.[119] An additional explanation is that, as Rosebery's name had been mentioned during the Queensberry trial, the government had Wilde arrested (and tried twice) in order to avoid giving the appearance of a Liberal cover-up.[120]

The alacrity and unanimity with which the Eighty Club hierarchy turned against their fellow member is likewise suggestive of cover-up and conspiracy. Asquith, Lockwood et al. may have pursued Wilde in order to protect themselves and the club's reputation. It is possible they were embarrassed at having given Wilde a prominent role in the organization by asking him to speak at an official event that was reported in the national press.

A little over a month after Wilde's conviction Rosebery delivered a speech to a club dinner which was attended by Charles Russell Junior, Asquith and Lockwood. We wonder if some of these men discussed, at some point during the evening, the Eighty Club member who was languishing in Pentonville Prison. Either way, the disgraced man would not be an embarrassment to the club hierarchy for much longer. Some months later Wilde's membership of the Eighty was declared void under rule 12(b), which related not to criminal convictions but to the non payment of subscription fees. This was an adroit solution which ensured there would be no lengthy internal discussion of the implications of Wilde's imprisonment for his membership. And so Wilde's long involvement with the Eighty Club ended not with an embarrassing bang (that might conceivably have reached the ears of the public) but with a whimper, his name being silently crossed out in its books.

Yet one member did not forget his erstwhile comrade. Richard Haldane, Vice President of the Eighty, served on the Gladstone Committee looking into prison conditions. In that capacity he had access to English jails. 'I used to meet [Wilde]', Haldane recalled years later, 'in the days of his social success, and, although I had not known him well, was haunted by the idea of what this highly sensitive man was probably suffering under ordinary prison treatment.' Haldane may have been referring here to his encounters with Wilde at Eighty Club events. It is also possible that Haldane spoke of those club meetings during a conversation he had with Wilde himself. For in the summer of 1895 Haldane decided to pay Wilde a friendly visit at Pentonville. When Haldane entered Wilde's cell, the prisoner at first refused to speak to him. 'I put my hand on his prison-dress-clad shoulder', wrote Haldane, 'and said that I used to know him'. These were the first sympathetic words Wilde had heard since his sentencing, and he burst into tears. Over the course of Wilde's two-year sentence Haldane helped the prisoner in numerous ways – procuring books for him, and arranging for transfers to prisons where he [Haldane] had friends among the staff.[121]

After his release from prison in 1897 Wilde acknowledged the kindness of the Eighty Club Vice President by sending him a copy of his poem *The Ballad of Reading Gaol* (1898). As *The Ballad* draws on the long tradition of Irish poetical protest, it is fitting that it should play a part in what was probably Wilde's last interaction with the club which he had joined out of commitment to the nationalist cause.[122]

Appendix: Timeline

This timeline includes Oscar Wilde's Eighty Club and nationalist activities for the years 1887 to 1895, and key events relating to the Liberal party and the 'Irish question'.

1885–1886 *winter* Gladstone converts to the Irish Home Rule cause.

1886 *summer* Liberal party splits into two factions – the Gladstonian Liberals and the Liberal Unionists, comprised of anti-Home Rule Radical and Whig MPs (the term 'Liberal Unionist' would be coined later).

June Gladstone's First Home Rule Bill falls at the second reading.

July The Tories and the Liberal Unionists gain a large majority at the general election.

1887 *early summer* Eighty Liberal Unionist members resign from the Eighty Club over its pro-Home Rule stance; on 29 June eighty candidates are elected to replace them (Wilde is likely to have been one of these new recruits). In total, 112 new members are recruited by the Eighty in 1887; the club is transformed into the think tank, and spiritual home, of pro-Home Rule Gladstonian Liberalism.

August The Tory Coercion Act is passed and vigorously implemented by Balfour, with the help of Carson.

September 21 Wilde makes a 'complimentary speech' following Justin McCarthy's lecture to the Southwark Irish Literary Club on 'the poets of '48'.
November 9 Wilde's nationalist and anti-Unionist review of J.P. Mahaffy's *Greek Life and Thought* is printed in the *PMG*.
December 13 Wilde attends his first club dinner, at which Lord Granville gives a speech about Ireland.
1888 *May 8* Wilde plans to attend, and may well have attended, a club dinner at which Parnell speaks on Irish matters.
July Wilde attends *The Times* vs Frank O'Donnell libel trial.
November 21 Wilde attends an Eighty Club at home.
1889 *early* Wilde attends an Eighty Club AGM to propose for membership Arthur Clifton, who is elected in July.
January 3 Wilde's review of Wilfrid Blunt's *In Vinculis*, which contains criticism of Tory coercion in Ireland, is printed in the *PMG*.
February 5 Wilde offers to help with the 'formation of a committee of National Protest' against 'the systematic injustice and inhumanity of Mr Balfour's rule in Ireland'.
February Wilde attends several sessions of the Parnell Commission.
March 8 Wilde attends an Eighty Club dinner at which Parnell speaks on Irish matters.
April 10 Wilde proposes a vote of thanks at an Eighty Club conversazione after a Liberal MP speaks about Ireland.
April 13 Wilde's nationalist review of J.A. Froude's Irish historical novel *Two Chiefs of Dunboy* is printed in the *PMG* under his initials – uniquely for one of Wilde's book reviews.
April 26 Wilde pays his Eighty Club subs.
July 3 Wilde attends the Eighty Club celebration of the Gladstones' golden wedding anniversary.
November 19 Wilde attends John Morley's Eighty Club lecture 'Liberalism and Social reforms' at London's St. James's Hall.

November 20 Wilde speaks at Gonville and Caius College, Cambridge, at a meeting of the Cambridge University Liberal Club, almost certainly as a representative of the Eighty Club.

1890 *February 27* Constance Wilde presides at a WLA meeting at which G.F.V. Knox, an Eighty Club member, speaks on 'Land Nationalisation'.

April 1 Wilde pays his Eighty Club subs.

May 14 Wilde attends a 'semi-political party' given by his friend, the Liberal MP Cyril Flower, for Eighty Club members. Constance accompanies him.

June 25 Wilde and about forty others attend an Eighty Club at home in the Westminster Palace Hotel.

November 25 Gladstone issues an ultimatum to Parnell in the wake of the O'Shea divorce scandal. Over the ensuing weeks the IPP splits into Parnellite and anti-Parnellite factions. Parnell subsequently turns against Gladstone. The chances of a Home Rule bill passing successfully through Westminster are reduced.

1891 *February* Wilde's political essay 'The Soul of Man under Socialism', which contains an unmistakable allusion to Parnell's downfall, is published in the February 1891 issue of the Liberal periodical *The Fortnightly Review*.

April 11 Wilde pays his Eighty Club subs.

April 17 Wilde attends an Eighty Club at home.

July 22 Wilde attends an Eighty Club at home hosted by the Liberal MP James Williamson.

October 6 Parnell dies.

1892 *January 5* Wilde pays his Eighty Club subs.

May 12 Wilde joins the Irish Literary Society.

June 15 Wilde attends another at home hosted by Cyril Flower. Constance again accompanies him. This appears to be the last club meeting Wilde attended.

July At the general election the Gladstonian Liberal and IPP coalition secure a small (45) seat majority.

1893 *July 10* Wilde pays his Eighty Club subs.

September The Liberal Second Home Rule Bill passes its third Commons reading, but is rejected by 378 votes in the Lords.

1894 *November 3* Wilde pays his Eighty Club subs.

1895 *mid–late* Wilde's club membership is declared void for non-payment of subs (on 25 May 1895 Wilde had been sentenced to two years' imprisonment for gross indecency).

Works cited

Allen, G., 'The Celt in English Art', *The Fortnightly Review* 55 (February 1891), pp. 267-277.
Atkinson, G.T., 'Oscar Wilde at Oxford', in E.H. Mikhail (ed.), *Oscar Wilde: Interviews and Recollections*, Vol. I (London & Basingstoke, 1979), pp. 15-20.
Beckett, J.C., *The Anglo-Irish Tradition* (London, 1976).
Bew, P., *C.S. Parnell* (Dublin, 1980).
Bristow, J. (ed.), *The Complete Works of Oscar Wilde, Vol. 3; The Picture of Dorian Gray: The 1890 and 1891 Texts* (Oxford, 2005).
—— *Oscar Wilde on Trial: The Criminal Proceedings, from Arrest to Imprisonment* (New Haven & London, 2022).
Callanan, F., *The Parnell Split 1890-91* (Syracuse, 1992).
Clayworth, A., 'Wilde the Irishman: the reclamation of a "recalcitrant patriot"', *The Wildean* 9 (July 1996), 28-31.
Coakley, D., 'Portrait of Oscar Wilde as an Irishman', in G. Franci & G. Silvani (ed.), *L'importanza di essere frainteso: omaggio a Oscar Wilde* [*The Importance of Being Misunderstood: Homage to Oscar Wilde*] (Bologna, 2001).
—— *Oscar Wilde: The Importance of Being Irish* (Dublin, 1994).
Cox, D. (ed.), *Constance Wilde's Autograph Book 1886-1896* (London, 2022).
Darnton, R., 'The dream of a universal library', *The New York Review of Books*, 21 December 2023, 73-74.

Donohue, J. (ed.), *The Complete Works of Oscar Wilde, Vol. 10: Plays, Vol. 3: The Importance of Being Earnest; 'A Wife's Tragedy' (fragment)* (Oxford, 2019).

Douglas, A., *Oscar Wilde and Myself* (London, 1914).

Dudley Edwards, O., 'Oscar Wilde and Henry O'Neill', *Irish Book Lover* 1, pp. 11–18.

—— 'The Soul of Man under Hibernicism', *Irish Studies Review* 11 (summer 1995), 7–13.

—— (ed.), *The Fireworks of Oscar Wilde* (London, 1989).

Dulau & Company Limited, *Catalogue 161: Oscar Wilde: Manuscripts, Autograph Letters, First Editions* (London, 1929).

Eagleton, T., *Scholars and Rebels in Nineteenth-Century Ireland* (Oxford, 1999).

Ellmann, R., *Oscar Wilde* (London, 1987).

Fahy, F., 'Ireland in London — Reminiscences (1921)', (ed. C. Hutton), in W.K. Chapman & W. Gould (ed.), *Yeats's Collaborations. Yeats Annual* 15: A Special Number (Basingstoke, 2002), pp. 233–280.

Fitzsimons, E. (ed.), *Articles from The Woman's World Edited by Oscar Wilde* (London, 2024).

Foster, R.F., *Modern Ireland 1600–1972* (London, 1988).

—— *Paddy and Mr Punch: Connections in Irish and English History* (London, 1993).

Frankel, N. (ed.), *The Picture of Dorian Gray: An Annotated, Uncensored Edition* (Cambridge, Mass., 2011).

Guy, J. (ed.), *The Complete Works of Oscar Wilde, Vol. 4: Criticism: Historical Criticism, Intentions, The Soul of Man* (Oxford, 2007).

—— (ed.), *The Complete Works of Oscar Wilde, Vol. 11: Plays, Vol. 4: Vera; or The Nihilist and Lady Windermere's Fan* (Oxford, 2021).

Haldane, R., *Autobiography* (London, 1929).

—— 'Various letters to the Governors of Pentonville and Wandsworth prisons, and to Ruggles-Brise, Chairman of the Prison Commission' (the Prison Commission file 8/432, Public Records Office, Kew, London).

Harris, F., *Oscar Wilde: His Life and Confessions* (New York, 1918).

Harrison, F., 'The Irish Leadership', *The Fortnightly Review*, January 1891, pp. 122–125.

Healy, T.M., *Letters and Leaders of my Day* (London, 1928).

Holland, M. (ed.), *Irish Peacock & Scarlet Marquess: The Real Trial of Oscar Wilde* (London, 2003).

Holland, M., & Hart-Davis, R. (ed.), *The Complete Letters of Oscar Wilde* (London, 2000).

Lewis, L., & Smith, H.J., *Oscar Wilde Discovers America* (New York, 1936).

Marez, C., 'The Other Addict: Reflections on Colonialism and Oscar Wilde's Opium Smoke Screen', *English Literary History* 64 (spring 1997), pp. 257–287.

Marjoribanks, E., *The Life of Lord Carson* (London, 1932).

Marland, R. (ed.), *Oscar Wilde: The Complete Interviews*, Volumes I & II (Jena, 2022).

Mason, S. [Millard, C.S.], *Bibliography of Oscar Wilde* (London, 1914).

Melville, J., *Mother of Oscar* (London, 1994).

Morley, J., *Liberalism & Social Reforms, 19th November, 1889. Speech by John Morley* (London, 1890).

Morris, R., Jr., *Declaring his Genius: Oscar Wilde in North America* (Cambridge, Mass., 2013).

Moyle, F., *Constance: The Tragic and Scandalous Life of Mrs Oscar Wilde* (London, 2011).

O'Brien, B., *The Life of Parnell* (London, 1898).

O'Connor, Mrs T.P., *I Myself* (London, 1910).

O'Neill, M.J., 'Irish Poets of the Nineteenth Century: Unpublished Lecture Notes of a speech by Oscar Wilde at San Francisco', *University Review* 1 (1955), pp. 29–32.

O'Sullivan, V., *Aspects of Wilde* (London, 1936).

Parnellism and Crime: The Special Commission Reprinted from 'The Times' (35 parts, 1888–1890).

Pearson, H., *The Life of Oscar Wilde* (London, 1946).

Pepper, R.D. (ed.), *Irish Poets and Poetry of the Nineteenth Century* (San Francisco, 1972).

Pulido, M.P., 'Lady Wilde "Speranza": A Woman of Great Importance', in C.G. Sandulescu (ed.), *Rediscovering Oscar Wilde* (Gerrards Cross, 1994), pp. 319–327.

Ross, R., 'Introduction' to *Reviews by Oscar Wilde* (London, 1908)

Sheehy, I., 'Irish Journalists and Littérateurs in Late Victorian London c.1870–1910' (D.Phil. thesis, Hertford College, University of Oxford, 2003), http://ora.ox.ac.uk/objects/uuid:5b952c75-ffc5-4dfb-bcac-7c749da5a722

Sherard, R.H., 'Is there Evidence of Survival?', *The Modern Mystic* 1, No. 4 (April–May 1937); University of Reading, RUL MS 1047, 4 (15).

Small, I. (ed.), *The Complete Works of Oscar Wilde, Vol. 8: The Short Fiction* (Oxford, 2017).

Stanford, W.B., & McDowell, R.B., *Mahaffy: A Biography of an Anglo-Irishman* (London, 1971).

Steven, R., *The National Liberal Club* (London, 1925).

Stokes, J., & Turner, M. (ed.), *The Complete Works of Oscar Wilde Volumes VI & VII: Journalism Parts I & II* (Oxford, 2013).

Sturgis, M., *Oscar: A Life* (London, 2018).

Taddei, A., 'London Clubs in the late Nineteenth Century', Discussion Papers in Economic and Social History Number 28, April 1999 (University of Oxford), http://www.economics.ox.

ac.uk/materials/papers/2264/28taddeiweb1.pdf accessed July 2015.

The Eighty Club 1880–1955: Seventy Five Years of Service (London, 1955).

The Eighty Club 1887 (London, 1887).

The Eighty Club 1888 (London, 1888).

The Eighty Club 1890 (London, 1891).

The Eighty Club 1891 (London, 1891).

The Eighty Club Account Book. Account Books for 1889–1892 and 1893–1896, Bodleian Library, Mss. Eng. d. 2017-8.

The Eighty Club Circular (December 1887).

The National Liberal Club: A Description with Illustrations (London, 1888).

Thévoz, S., '1886–1916: The Birth and Growth of Cambridge University Liberal Club', *Journal of Liberal History* 91 (summer 2016), pp. 10–22.

Tipper, K.S.A., *A Critical Biography of Lady Jane Wilde, 1821?–1896: Irish Revolutionist, Humanist, Scholar and Poet* (Lewiston, Queenston, Lampeter, 2002).

—— (ed.), *Lady Jane Wilde's Letters to Froken Lotten Von Kraemer, 1857–1885* (Lewiston, Queenston, Lampeter, 2009).

—— (ed.), *Lady Jane Wilde's Letters to Oscar Wilde, 1875–1895: A Critical Edition* (Lewiston, Queenston, Lampeter, 2011).

Tite Street Catalogue…, (London, 1895).

Walshe, E., *Oscar's Shadow: Wilde, Homosexuality and Modern Ireland* (Cork, 2012).

Wilde, [Jane] Lady, 'The American Irish', *Ancient Cures, Charms and Usages of Ireland* (London, 1890).

Wright, T., 'Oscar Wilde: Hellenism', *The Wildean* 41 (July 2012), pp. 1–50.

—— 'The Complete Works of Oscar Wilde: Volumes VI & VII', *The Wildean* 44 (January 2014), pp. 115–137.

—— 'Party Political Animal: Oscar Wilde. Gladstonian Liberal and Eighty Club Member', *Times Literary Supplement*, 6 June 2014, pp. 13–15.

Wyse Jackson, J., *Oscar Wilde in Saint Louis* (Missouri, 2012).

Yeats, W.B., *Autobiographies* (London, 1955).

—— (ed.), *A Book of Irish Verse* (London, 1895).

Notes

1. https://archive.org/details/oscar-wilde-a-parnellite-home-ruler-and-gladstonian-liberal; https://hcommons.org/deposits/item/hc:69343; https://www.academia.edu/123937570

2. Darnton, R., 'The dream of a universal library', *The New York Review of Books*, 21 December 2023, 73-74.

3. We have previously written or spoken about our findings on three occasions – in an essay: Thomas Wright, 'Party Political Animal: Oscar Wilde. Gladstonian Liberal and Eighty Club Member', *Times Literary Supplement*, 6 June 2014, pp. 13-15; in a conference paper: Paul Kinsella, 'Oscar Wilde's Irish nationalism and his views on English party politics: Some new evidence', given at the 'Wilde Days in Paris 2014' conference (Centre Cultural Irlandais, 11-14 June, 2014); and in an earlier version of this essay, which was published in August-September 2015 in the 'May I say nothing?' section of the now defunct Oscholars website. This latest version of the essay was revised in 2024.

4. We know Wilde joined in 1887 because the first club members list in which his name appears is the one for that year (published in *The Eighty Club 1888* (London, 1888), p. 4). The time lag between the proposal and election of a candidate was at least a few months so we can assume Wilde decided to join the club, and was first proposed as a candidate, in the summer of 1887 at the latest. Wilde's decision was probably made earlier than this, in the spring of 1887 at the latest, as the most likely date for his election is 29 June 1887 (see p. 6 above). Unless a candidate was directly elected by the club's committee (and Wilde was not one of the candidates thus elected in 1887) he was first proposed, at a general meeting of the club, by an existing member who knew him well, then seconded by at least one other member who could vouch for his character

(both the proposer and seconder had to be 'personally acquainted' with the candidate). At the next general meeting he was balloted, one black ball in nine being enough to exclude him from election. Elections took place four times a year. A number of Wilde's friends and professional colleagues might have proposed and seconded his candidature, including E.T. Cook, the MPs Charles Dilke, Cyril Flower and William Grenfell, and two members of the Verney family, all of whom were club members at the start of 1887. Wilde's acquaintances George Macmillan, Justin H. McCarthy and Lord Houghton all joined the club at some point in 1887 so they might conceivably have been involved in his election. This seems unlikely however given the strong probability that they were elected on the same occasion as Wilde.

5. *The Eighty Club 1888*, pp. 3–5.

6. *The Eighty Club 1887* (London, 1887), p. 9. *The Eighty Club 1888* (London, 1888, pp. 9–10), and Steven, R., *The National Liberal Club* (London, 1925), pp. 21–22.

7. *The Eighty Club Circular* (December, 1887), p. 1.

8. The 'Plan of Campaign' referred to the strategy, developed by William O'Brien and others, whereby 'dissatisfied tenants on particular estates ... [combined] ... to offer the landlord their notion of a fair rent. If it was refused, they paid him nothing; instead they contributed the proposed sum to an estate fund which would be employed for the protection of tenants in the event of landlord retaliation.' Paul Bew, *C.S. Parnell* (Dublin, 1980), pp. 97–98.

9. Frankel, N. (ed.), *The Picture of Dorian Gray: An Annotated, Uncensored Edition* (Cambridge, Mass., 2011), p. 142 n4.

10. Stokes, J., & Turner, M. (ed.), *The Complete Works of Oscar Wilde Volumes VI & VII: Journalism Parts I & II* (Oxford, 2013); *Journalism I*, pp. xxiv–xxv & p. xxix. E.T. Cook (assistant editor of the *PMG* and one of Wilde's contacts at the paper) was a member of the Eighty Club, as was Cassell's manager Wemyss Reid, who appointed Wilde to the editorship of the *Lady's World* (which then became the *Woman's World*).

11. Wilde also visited several London clubs at this time as a guest. For the social and economic benefits of club membership see Taddei, A., 'London Clubs in the late Nineteenth Century', *Discussion Papers in Economic and Social History*, Number 28, April 1999 (University of Oxford), http://www.

economics.ox.ac.uk/materials/ papers/2264/28taddeiweb1.pdf accessed July 2015. Taddei writes: 'Club membership provided a ready-made means for social intercourse, an information network, and a source of societal status... clubs facilitated the development of a network of mutually profitable semi-professional acquaintances' (pp. 15-16). However, as Taddei suggests, the Eighty Club was, relatively speaking, of limited usefulness for those who wanted to establish gentlemanly status, and to make social contacts. It is revealing, in this context, to compare the Eighty Club's official objectives (quoted in the previous section), with those of the National Liberal Club, whose principal aim was to 'provide a central, convenient, and inexpensive club in London for Liberals throughout the Kingdom, at which they may obtain every comfort and club advantage, where they may meet in friendly intercourse, and exchange information and views' (*The National Liberal Club: A Description with Illustrations* (London, 1888)). This reveals the overtly political ethos of the Eighty in comparison with the National Liberal Club (we may also recall here that MPs and would-be MPs comprised a large proportion of its membership). It is, moreover, illuminating to compare the responses of the two clubs to the schism in the party over Home Rule – see pp. 6-8 above. Unlike many Eighty Clubbers, Wilde did not join the National Liberal Club, despite the fact that a number of his friends and acquaintances were members.

12. *The Eighty Club Circular* (London), December 1887, p. 8.

13. *The Eighty Club 1888*, p. 5; club rule 7b also reads: 'No candidate shall be proposed for election by the club unless he shall have signified to his proposer that he is willing to take part in political work on behalf of the Liberal Party' (*ibid.*)

14. Atkinson, G.T., 'Oscar Wilde at Oxford', in Mikhail, E.H. (ed.), *Oscar Wilde: Interviews and Recollections* (London & Basingstoke, 1979), Vol. I, p. 19.

15. Holland, M., & Hart-Davis, R. (ed.), *The Complete Letters of Oscar Wilde* (London, 2000), p. 606. Michael J. O'Neill, 'Irish Poets of the Nineteenth Century: Unpublished Lecture Notes of a speech by Oscar Wilde at San Francisco', *University Review* 1 (1955), p. 30. Ellmann, R., *Oscar Wilde* (London, 1987), pp. 5-8. Among Wilde's favourite Speranza poems were her ballad on the trial and execution of the Sheares Brothers for having 'sought to free their land from thrall of stranger' during the 1798 rebellion, and 'Courage', also written in 'the

year of revolution'. (Pepper, R.D (ed.), *Irish Poets and Poetry of the Nineteenth Century* (San Francisco, 1972), p. 33.)

16. *Irish Poets and Poetry of the Nineteenth Century*, p. 32.

17. Coakley, D., *Oscar Wilde: The Importance of Being Irish* (Dublin, 1994), p. 94. It seems that Sir William's dreams of joining the nobility were not realised, at least in the eyes of some Irishmen. W.B. Yeats, for example, would call Wilde 'a parvenu, but a parvenu whose whole bearing proved that if he did dedicate every story in *A House of Pomegranates* to a lady of title, it was but to show that he was Jack and the social ladder his pantomime beanstalk' (*Autobiographies* (London, 1955), pp. 138-139), and George Moore, the son of an Irish landowner, seems to have 'looked down on the son of the Dublin practitioner'. (O'Sullivan, V., *Aspects of Wilde* (London, 1936), p. 102.) Apropos of the Anglo-Irish middle-class's precarious socio-political position in Ireland David Lloyd comments: '[its members were] deracinated with regard to rural and Gaelic Ireland and only recentered awkwardly with regard to the Empire, on whose political power they [were] socially economically and culturally parasitic but from whose center they [were] none the less excluded.' Lloyd, D., *Nationalism and Minor Literature:* *James Clarence Mangan and the Emergence of Irish Cultural Nationalism* (Berkeley, 1987), p. 61, quoted in Marez, C., 'The Other Addict: Reflections on Colonialism and Oscar Wilde's Opium Smoke Screen', *English Literary History* 64 (Spring 1997), pp. 257-287.

18. Beckett, J.C., *The Anglo-Irish Tradition* (London, 1976), p. 10. Yet, at the same time, many members of the caste so identified as Irish that they did not feel much sympathy with the English, and so often bit the imperial hand that protected them. As John Butler Yeats put it 'we [Anglo-Irish] intended as good Protestants to keep the papists under our feet ... yet we were convinced that an Irishman, whether Protestant or Catholic, was superior to every Englishman.' (Quoted in Stanford, W.B., & McDowell, R.B., *Mahaffy: A Biography of an Anglo-Irishman* (London, 1971), p. 120.)

19. In this context, it is interesting to read W.B. Yeats' description of Young Ireland poetry in the preface and introduction to his *A Book of Irish Verse*. Yeats comments: 'The Young Ireland writers wrote to give the peasantry a literature in English in place of the literature they were losing with Gaelic...' *A Book of Irish Verse*, pp. xiii-xiv & pp. xviii-xix. It is also worth

noting that Oscar may have been baptized twice – first as a Protestant and then as a Catholic – and that he was drawn to the Roman faith throughout his adult life. See Mason, S., *Bibliography of Oscar Wilde* (London, 1914), p. 118.

20. Wilde, W., *Irish Popular Superstitions* (Dublin, 1852); Wilde, J.F., *Ancient Legends, Mystic Charms, and Superstitions of Ireland* (London, 1887); and Wilde, J. F., *Ancient Cures, Charms, and Usages of Ireland* (London, 1890).

21. For Sir William's views see Tipper, K.S.A., *A Critical Biography of Lady Jane Wilde, 1821?–1896: Irish Revolutionist, Humanist, Scholar and Poet* (Lewiston, Queenston, Lampeter, 2002), pp. 530–536. For Speranza's ambivalent views see her pamphlet *The American Irish* (Dublin, n.d.), which has been variously dated between 1877 and 1879. This work, which discusses the influence of the American Irish on the nationalist movement, was republished as an essay ('The American Irish') in Speranza's book *Ancient Cures, Charms and Usages of Ireland* (London, 1890), which is the source of all quotations in our essay (her ambivalent views about the British Empire are aired there on pp. 243–244). The Wildes' ambivalence on the constitutional question is by no means exceptional. It is difficult to accurately define the views of many Irish nationalists (including nationalist leaders, such as Parnell) on the precise constitutional form 'independence' or 'separation' from England ought to take, or to gauge they extent to which they saw Home Rule as a stepping stone towards complete independence.

22. 'Letter undated to unknown correspondent', quoted in Pulido, M.P., 'Lady Wilde "Speranza": A Woman of Great Importance', in C.G. Sandulescu (ed.), *Rediscovering Oscar Wilde* (Gerrards Cross, 1994), p. 322.

23. Letter of ?1866, repr. in Tipper, K.S.A. (ed.), *Lady Jane Wilde's Letters to Froken Lotten Von Kraemer, 1857–1885* (Lewiston, Queenston, Lampeter, 2009), p. 43. Speranza expressed support for an Irish republic in *The American Irish*, p. 204 & p. 241. The Anglo-Irish snobbery informing some of Speranza's remarks was also detected behind some of her son's statements and his general behaviour (see, for example, *Aspects of Wilde*, p. 78). The Wildes' snobbishness may not be entirely unrelated to their uncertain position within the Anglo-Irish élite, as middle-class professionals aspiring to gentry status, as well as to the uncertain position of the Anglo-Irish élite itself.

24. Eagleton, T., *Scholars and Rebels in Nineteenth-Century Ireland* (Oxford, 1999), p. 26.

25. Foster, R.F., 'Parnell and His People' in *Paddy and Mr Punch: Connections in Irish and English History* (London, 1993), p. 63 & p. 76.

26. 'The American Irish', in *Ancient Cures*, p. 240.

27. Wilde made these comments in 1881 while recommending the pamphlet to an editor of an English periodical (*Complete Letters*, pp. 115-116). However, as Wilde kept abreast of his mother's publications (and also reportedly edited his mother's prose on occasion while it was still in manuscript) he is likely to have read *The American Irish* either before or soon after its appearance in print towards the end of the 1870s. Robert Ross mentions Wilde's editorial involvement in his mother's writings in a letter he wrote to Walter Ledger, 11 December 1907 (University College Oxford Library, Robert Ross Memorial Collection, 'The letters of Robert Ross to Walter Ledger 1902-1918, MS Ross 4).

28. *Irish Times*, 25 May 1877, p. 6.

29. See Dudley Edwards, O., 'Oscar Wilde and Henry O'Neill', *Irish Book Lover*, Vol. I, pp. 11-18. Wilde's appeal was reprinted in *The Nation*, the nationalist newspaper for which Speranza had written in her Young Ireland days.

30. Sherard, R.H., 'Is there Evidence of Survival?', *The Modern Mystic* 1, No. 4 (April-May 1937). We believe it is no coincidence that, once Wilde had established himself in England, he had no hesitation in asserting his Irishness publically as well as privately, and that he also became increasingly outspoken on Irish political issues. It is interesting to note that in nineteenth-century England, the Irish were often caricatured as uncultivated, apish, violent, sentimental, dirty, feckless, incapable of self-government, childish, and impractical, and that Wilde (along with other Irishmen in late nineteenth-century London, including Parnell, Shaw and Yeats) created a persona that contradicted this racial stereotype in every respect.

31. *Irish Poets and Poetry of the Nineteenth Century*, p. 18.

32. *Daily Globe* (Saint Paul), 18 March 1882, p. 1.

33. *Irish Poets and Poetry of the Nineteenth Century*, p. 28 & p. 34. Speranza told her son that she was 'greatly interested in all the San Francisco

[news]papers', Tipper, K.S.A. (ed.), *Lady Jane Wilde's Letters to Oscar Wilde, 1875–1895: A Critical Edition* (Lewiston, Queenston, Lampeter, 2011), p. 75.

34. The only substantial commentary on the interview appears in Jackson, J.W., *Oscar Wilde in Saint Louis* (Missouri, 2012). Jackson characterises the nationalist views Wilde expresses in it as 'advanced and radical' (p. 74). Roy Morris Jr. also mentions the interview in *Declaring his Genius: Oscar Wilde in North America* (Cambridge, Mass., 2013), pp. 167–168. It was recently reprinted in Marland, R. (ed.), *Oscar Wilde: The Complete Interviews* (Jena, 2022), Vol. I, pp. 222–226.

35. In 1880 the Land League's Land War campaign began, during which it agitated for the so-called Three Fs (fair rent, fixity of tenure and free sale of land), by coordinating resistance to tenant evictions and by boycotting landlords who demanded high rents, along with the tenants who paid them. Ultimately, the League believed that the land should be transferred from the landlords to the tenantry and peasantry, though opinions differed as to how this might be carried out. Davitt advocated a programme of land nationalisation, adopting as his slogan 'The land of Ireland for the people of Ireland'. The League was well known throughout America because Davitt, and other leaders, had given speeches there in 1878 and 1879, and collected money for their campaign from Irish Americans (Davitt would return to America in June 1882, while Wilde was still lecturing).

36. Wilde (who had settled in London around 1879 after completing his Oxford degree) used reduced income from rent as an excuse for not settling his bills in the English capital (see *Complete Letters*, p. 84). For Speranza's problems in collecting rent from the Wildes' land and property in the West of Ireland, and the attendant difficulties this created, see Melville, J., *Mother of Oscar* (London, 1994), p. 170 & p. 178.

37. The wealth and power of Anglo-Irish landlords was, Parnell believed, 'the strongest inducement to [them] to uphold the system of English misrule'. Only when this inducement had been removed would the Anglo-Irish caste support the nationalist movement and indeed become 'the natural and effective, and safe leaders of the people'. See *C.S. Parnell*, pp. 45–46.

38. *Mother of Oscar Wilde*, p. 178.

39. Lewis, L., & Smith, H.J., *Oscar Wilde Discovers America* (New York, 1936), p. 215. 'Parnell also he admired

.... Parnell he put higher [than Disraeli] because he led a people' (*Aspects of Wilde*, p. 80 & p. 222). Wilde was impressed by Parnell's aristocratic hauteur, as well as by the imperiousness with which he exercised control over the IPP in Westminster. He regaled his friends with anecdotes illustrating these qualities, which suggest insider knowledge of the workings of the Irish party. 'One night', he told Vincent O'Sullivan, 'when the Irish had won an important division amid the wildest excitement, [Tim Healy] turned to Parnell and shouted: "Sure, it's a great night for Ireland, Parnell!" "Mr Parnell, I suppose you mean", replied the calm Parnell freezingly.' (*Aspects of Wilde*, p. 222). So far as Wilde was concerned Parnell's aristocratic background made him infinitely preferable as leader of the IPP to another candidate for that role in the early eighties – the middle-class Joseph Biggar, a Belfast butcher-turned-politician. Of Biggar's candidature Wilde remarked, 'I can *never* consent to be led by – a bacon merchant!' (*The Importance of Being Irish*, p. 197.) It is possible that Wilde also admired Parnell's 'disregard for the social and sexual *mores*' of middle-class Victorian England, the chief's relationship with the married Katherine O'Shea having been gossiped about in London circles from 1881 onwards (*C.S. Parnell*, pp. 42–43). When it was made public, at the end of 1889, the press heaped scorn on Parnell, but he remained defiant and nonchalant. To English eyes then Parnell was, like Wilde, both a nationalist and a sexual rebel.

40. Wilde was also referring to the profound influence of Irish Americans on the Land League's ideas and organisation generally. In an interview given a month later he spoke of the League as 'the most remarkable agitation that has ever taken place in Ireland, for it has, through the influence of America, created a Republican feeling in Ireland for the first time. The agitations that preceded it, would, if successful, have resulted in the establishment of a monarchy. Now, success would mean the foundation of a republic.' (*San Francisco Chronicle*, 27 March 1882, p. 3, repr. in *Complete Interviews*, Vol. I, p. 296–303). Not for the last time, Wilde was echoing the argument of his mother's *The American Irish*, which predicts that American Republicanism will inspire Irish nationalism. John Wyse Jackson suggests Wilde had a copy of Speranza's pamphlet with him during his American Lecture tour, and that it informs some of the statements on Irish politics he made there (Jackson, p.73). This seems likely given the way he echoed it in his San Francisco lecture. Wilde said, 'There is ... one art which

no tyranny can kill and no penal laws can stifle, the art of poetry ... The poetry of the Irish people... kept alive the fires of patriotism in the hearts of the Irish people' (*Irish Poets and Poetry of the Nineteenth Century*, p. 27). This recalls Speranza's comment: 'All oppressed nations are eloquent. When laws forbid a people to arm, they can only speak or sing.' (p. 199.) Echoes of Speranza's pamphlet would also appear in Wilde's 1889 *PMG* review of J.A. Froude's *The Two Chiefs of Dunboy* (*Journalism I*, pp. 203-206). For example where Speranza wrote 'the American Irish are now powerful enough to command success. They have become a great and mighty people in the land of their adoption — a nation greater than the nation at home ... exile ... seems to intensify their feelings' (p. 200 & p. 204), Wilde commented 'To mature its powers, to concentrate its action, to learn the secret of its own strength ... the Celtic intellect has had to cross the Atlantic. At home it had but learned the pathetic weakness of nationality; in a strange land it realized what indomitable forces nationality possesses. What captivity was to the Jews, exile has been to the Irish.' (*Journalism II*, p. 203.) In his review Wilde also describes Parnell as Ireland's 'first practical leader' (Ibid.), and this recalls his description of his mother's pamphlet as an essay 'on the reflux wave of practical republicanism which the return of the Irish emigrants has brought on Ireland' (*Complete Letters*, pp. 115-116).

41. 'You know Parnell, Sullivan and McCarthy?' Wilde was asked. This is a reference to T.D. Sullivan and Justin McCarthy. Sullivan was an IPP MP and the author of the Irish national hymn 'God Save Ireland'; he owned and edited a number of nationalist papers such as *The Nation* and *Young Ireland*. McCarthy was a writer and prominent IPP member. He and Wilde often met socially.

42. Veteran Young Irelanders and Irish politicians such as Frank Hugh O'Donnell and Phillip Callan attended Speranza's salons. Speranza makes an enthusiastic reference to O'Donnell and Callan in a letter she wrote to Oscar on 8 May 1882 (*Lady Jane Wilde's Letters to Oscar Wilde, 1875-1895: A Critical Edition*, p. 77. A reference to a discussion about the Land League appears in *Mother of Oscar*, p. 178). It is possible that Parnell himself attended one of Speranza's salons, or that Wilde met him through one of her political acquaintances. Drawing on an earlier version of our essay, Matthew Sturgis discusses Oscar's Irish politics in his *Oscar: A Life* (London, 2018), pp. 358-359 & p. 805 n40.

43. Wilde echoed these comments on a later occasion when he remarked that 'the case of the South in the civil war was to my mind much like that of Ireland today. It was a struggle for autonomy, self-government for a people. I do not wish to see the empire dismembered, but only to see the Irish people free, and Ireland still as a willing and integral part of the British Empire. To dismember a great empire in this age of vast armies and overweening ambition on the part of other nations, is to consign the peoples of the broken country to weak and insignificant places in the panorama of nations; but people must have freedom and autonomy before they are capable of their greatest result in the cause of progress. This is my feeling about the Southern people, as it is about my own people, the Irish.' (*The Daily Picayune* (New Orleans), 25 June 1882, p. 11, repr. in *Complete Interviews*, Vol. I, pp. 431–433.)

44. Parnell uttered these famous words in Cork on 21 January 1885 (quoted in *C.S. Parnell*, p. 70). It is difficult to pin down exactly what kind of settlement Parnell envisaged for an 'independent' Ireland or to understand whether he imagined it maintaining at least some ties with the British Empire. The ambivalence, and indistinctness of his views, may help us understand how a patriotic Home Ruler such as Wilde could sometimes express admiration for the British Empire and for Queen Victoria, despite defining himself as a 'thorough republican' (Ellmann, *Oscar Wilde*, p. 186). For an interesting discussion of some of Wilde's views on imperialism see 'The Other Addict: Reflections on Colonialism and Oscar Wilde's Opium Smoke Screen'. [op.cit.]

45. Wilde may also have been thinking of the Irish uprising of '48 here which, as we have seen, he described as an 'unsuccessful rebellion'. Wilde's ambiguous attitude to violent revolution is later echoed in 'The Soul of Man under Socialism' where he writes, 'The very violence of a revolution may make the public grand and splendid for a moment' (Guy, J. (ed.), *The Complete Works of Oscar Wilde, Vol. 4: Criticism: Historical Criticism, Intentions, The Soul of Man* (Oxford, 2007), 254.27–28).

46. 'The American Irish', *Ancient Cures*, p. 232 & p. 243. Gladstone made his famous declaration in a speech concerning the Bulgarian peoples struggle to be free from Turkish tyranny. Wilde wrote a poem on this subject entitled 'On the recent massacres of the Christians in Bulgaria', which he sent to the Liberal leader. (*Complete Letters*, p. 46.)

47. 'It is very strange', Wilde continued, 'that in the House of Commons you never hear the word "Civilization" ... there is seldom a piece of legislation that does not benefit one class more than another; and that perhaps makes the wretched party spirit more bitter' (this last remark may be a veiled allusion to the 1881 Irish Land Act, which suggests that Wilde's apparent apathy towards the English parties had a specific, Irish cause). However, Wilde also stated that 'Gladstone is the greatest Prime Minister England ever had'. (*Philadelphia Press*, 17 January 1882, p. 2, repr. in *Complete Interviews*, Vol. I, pp. 70–78).

48. 'What! Thomas Burke assassinated!' Wilde exclaimed, 'The friend of my father, and he who has so often dined at our house! And Lord Cavendish, too! I do not see why they should wish to assassinate mediocrity, for he was just an easy-going, pleasant, mediocre gentleman whom no one could have a grudge against. Such, too, was Mr. Burke ... I am very sorry to hear the news, and hope it isn't true'. Wilde then suggested the attacks were 'undoubtedly the result of intoxication at what the Irish thought a complete victory' – a reference to the fact that Parnell and other Land League leaders had, a few days previously, been released by the Liberal government from prison. 'They turned liberty into license', Wilde continued, and 'when liberty comes with hands dabbled in blood it is hard to shake hands with her, eh?' (*Chicago Sunday Tribune*, 7 May 1882, p. 3, repr. in *Complete Interviews*, Vol. I, p. 386–388.) When confronted by news of terrorist murder it seems that Wilde was unable to maintain the scientific historical perspective on events in Ireland which he had adopted during his *Globe Democrat* interview.

49. *Chicago Sunday Tribune*, 7 May 1882, p. 3, repr. in *Complete Interviews*, Vol. I, p. 386–388

50. *Complete Letters*, p. 266.

51. *Journalism II*, p. 241. this comment was made in the Liberal periodical *The Speaker* whose editor was Wemyss Reid. While this article was signed by Wilde, most of his *PMG* reviews were anonymous, though, presumably, some of literary and journalistic London would have been aware of his authorship, on account of their views and style.

52. *Journalism II*, p. 12. Wilde's comments on William O'Brien were printed on 9 November 1887, four days before 10,000 protestors marched on Trafalgar Square to demonstrate against O'Brien's imprisonment and against coercion generally (along with

other grievances such as high unemployment). The protest was organised by the Irish National League and the Social Democratic Federation. Around 2500 policemen and soldiers attempted to halt the march and violence ensued, after which 400 people were arrested and 50 detained. The incident became known as Bloody Sunday. Among those arrested were the Liberal Home Rule politician, Robert Cunninghame-Graham and the radical John Burns, both of whom Wilde knew. When they were charged at Bow Street police court on 14 November 1887 Wilde attended the proceedings (*PMG*, 15 November 1887, p. 7).

53. *Journalism II*, pp. 12–15, p. 67, pp. 149–152, & p. 231. It is interesting to note that Wilde also frequently criticized the Tory Press at this time. In 1889 he wrote to W.E. Henley, editor of *The Scots Observer*: 'To be exiled to Scotland to edit a Tory paper ... is bad ...' (*Complete Letters*, p. 409). In his appraisal of J.P. Mahaffy's *Greek Life and Thought*, printed on 9 November 1887, Wilde castigates his former Trinity College classics tutor for the 'silliness and bad taste' with which he abdicates his responsibility as a 'true historian' by using a discussion of ancient history to promote his 'Paper-Unionist' views. '[I]n his attempts', writes Wilde, 'to treat the Hellenic world as "Tipperary writ large" ... Mr. Mahaffy shows an amount of political bias and literary blindness that is quite extraordinary.' In other words history, like art or science, should be objective, and Mahaffy has betrayed his calling by tainting his book with prejudice. Yet because Mahaffy's views are repugnant and outrageous to Wilde, he takes a thinly-disguised relish in his attack. Wilde also feels justified in fighting the author on his own Irish political ground. 'Mr. Balfour is very anxious', he writes, 'that Mr. William O'Brien should wear prison clothes, sleep on a plank bed, and be subjected to other indignities, but Mr. Mahaffy goes far beyond such mild measures ... by frankly expressing his regret that Demosthenes was not summarily put to death for his attempts to keep the spirit of patriotism alive among the citizens of Athens!' Wilde also makes a pointed reference to Michelstown, scene of O'Brien's conviction and of the police murder of three protesters who demonstrated against his trial. Wilde launches these political missiles in passing, as he moves from his principal objection to Mahaffy's book to his review's other great theme – a historical counter argument concerning 'the political value of autonomy and the intellectual importance of a healthy national life' in Ancient Greece, which, Wilde says, is sup-

ported by 'the facts of history', and he challenges Mahaffy to deny these (*Journalism II*, 12–15). Wilde had developed this argument, which has obvious Irish political overtones, as an undergraduate. See Wright, T., 'Oscar Wilde: Hellenism', *The Wildean*, 41 (July 2012), pp. 1–50, especially pp. 18–21. For the political background to Wilde's review of Mahaffy's book see Coakley, D., 'Portrait of Oscar Wilde as an Irishman', in G. Franci & G. Silvani (ed.), *L'importanza di essere frainteso: omaggio a Oscar Wilde* [*The Importance of Being Misunderstood: Homage to Oscar Wilde*] (Bologna, 2001), pp. 309–322. Wilde's appraisal of Mahaffy's book is typical of his reviews. As a rule, he endeavoured to separate politics from history or literature, and to concentrate on the formal and intellectual aspects of the work under consideration. In other words, Wilde generally tried to read books as an aesthete and as a thinker first and as a nationalist second. That said, it is apparent, from his reviews of Mahaffy, Swinburne, *et al.*, that Wilde found it hard to resist lambasting authors who promoted opinions he opposed. Thus he cannot help taking the following swipes at John Cameron Grant: '[he] has christened himself "England's Empire Poet," and, lest we should have any doubts upon the subject, tells us that he "dare not lie," a statement which in a poet seems to show a great want of courage. Protection and Paper-Unionism are the gods of Mr. Grant's idolatry, and his verse is full of such fine fallacies and masterly misrepresentations that he should be made Laureate to the Primrose League [A Tory organization] at once ... it would be difficult for the advocates of Coercion to find a more appropriate or a more characteristic peroration for a stump speech than "We have not to do with justice, right depends on point of view, [/] The one question for our thought is, what's our neighbour going to do." ... and the sonnet on Mr. Gladstone is sure to be popular with all who admire violence and vulgarity in literature. It is quite worthy of Thersites at his best' (*Journalism II*, p. 67). Similarly Wilde found it difficult to contain his anger when any English writers he reviewed depicted the Irish in prejudiced, stereotypical and vulgar ways – e.g. 'The Celtic element in literature is extremely valuable', Wilde comments, in a review of George Dalziel's verse, 'but there is absolutely no excuse for shrieking "Shillelagh!" and "O'Gorrah!"' (*Journalism II*, p. 53.) The editors of the OET *Journalism* volumes attribute to Wilde another anonymous book review with an Irish theme – a review of Lady Wilde's *Ancient Legends, Mystic Charms, and Superstitions of Ireland* published on 19 February 1887 in the *PMG* (*Journalism*

I, pp. 125-128). However, we believe this piece cannot be by Wilde for the reasons set out in Wright, T., 'The Complete Works of Oscar Wilde: Volumes VI & VII', *The Wildean* 44 (January 2014), pp. 115-137.

54. Stokes and Turner describe *The Woman's World* as 'reformist and broadly Liberal, reflecting Wilde's own political sympathies' (*Journalism I*, p. xxxvii); they also remark on the Liberal persuasion of most of the papers and magazines to which Wilde contributed.

55. *The Woman's World*, Vol. 2, January 1889, pp. 140-143, repr. in Fitzsimons, E. (ed.), *Articles from The Woman's World Edited by Oscar Wilde* (London, 2024), pp. 89-93. In 1888 for example Wilde printed an essay on Dublin Castle which condemned the 'hideous savagery' of Cromwell, as well as several articles promoting Irish industries, in the course of which a bleak picture of rural Ireland is painted.

56. Small, I. (ed.), *The Complete Works of Oscar Wilde, Vol. 8: The Short Fiction* (Oxford, 2017), 51.4-11. For example, in his first social comedy, *Lady Windermere's Fan* (1893), the heroine Mrs Erlynne flatters a fellow party guest by saying: 'I am so much interested in [your nephew's] political career. I think he's sure to be a wonderful success. He thinks like a Tory and talks like a Radical, and that's so important now-a-days.' (Guy, J. (ed.), *The Complete Works of Oscar Wilde, Vol. 11: Plays, Vol. 4: Vera; or The Nihilist and Lady Windermere's Fan* (Oxford, 2021), 487.211-213). Wilde echoes the joke in his next comedy, *A Woman of No Importance* (1894), which features Mr Kelvil, an MP who espouses views of a distinctly Radical cast but turns out to be a hypocrite. As Kelvil is also a prig he may have reminded the play's first audiences of Joseph Chamberlain, the most prominent Radical Liberal Unionist, who espoused puritanical causes such as temperance.

57. For more information on the Southwark Irish Literary Club see Ian Sheehy, 'Irish Journalists and Littérateurs in Late Victorian London c.1870-1910' (D.Phil. thesis, Hertford College, University of Oxford, 2003), http://ora.ox.ac.uk/objects/uuid:5b9 52c75-ffc5-4dfb-bcac-7c749da5a722. We gratefully acknowledge the help and advice Dr Sheehy has given us during our research into the historical background for this essay.

58. It is possible though that Wilde reprised some of the comments he had made on Young Ireland during his San Francisco lecture 'Irish Poets and Poetry of the Nineteenth Century'. This is suggested by the re-emergence,

in 1919, of a 'typescript of a lecture delivered by [Wilde] at the Southwark Literary Society, London, with two corrections in his handwriting. The lecture deals with the leaders of the '48 movement, and has not been published'. The typescript was offered for sale in W.G. Neale's *Catalogue of first editions, April 1919* [W.G. Neale, 12 Aston's Quay, Dublin.], a copy of which is in the Robert Ross Memorial Collection, University College Oxford Library (Ross e. 628). The current whereabouts of this typescript is unknown. It may also be worth noting that, in its account of the evening, *Freeman's Journal and Daily Commercial Advertiser* (23 September 1887, p. 4) referred to Wilde's contribution as a 'speech'. On the other hand, though, most surviving accounts of Wilde's speech do not give the impression that he spoke at great length.

59. *Freeman's Journal and Daily Commercial Advertister*, 23 September 1887, p. 4; *PMG*, 22 September 1887, p. 7; *The South London Press*, 24 September 1887; and Hutton, C. (ed.), 'Francis Fahy's "Ireland in London — Reminiscences" (1921)', in W.K. Chapman & W. Gould (ed.), *Yeats's Collaborations. Yeats Annual* 15: A Special Number (Basingstoke, 2002), p. 250. In referring to Speranza in this context Wilde was publically identifying himself as the inheritor of her views – as he had done during his American lecture tour.

60. *The Times*, 14 December 1887, p. 6.

61. The William Andrews Clark Junior Memorial Library, Los Angeles, possesses Wilde's copy of *The Eighty Club 1891* (London, 1891) (PR5828. E34). We would like to thank the former Head Librarians Dr Gerald Cloud and Bruce Whiteman, for allowing Thomas Wright to consult the item; he would also like to thank Suzanne Tatian and Scott Jacobs, librarians at the Clark. This pamphlet was purchased by William Andrews Clark Jr. at the 1928 'Dulau Sale' of Wilde material 'formerly in the possession of [Robert] Ross, [Christopher] Millard and the younger son of Oscar Wilde'. Dulau & Company Limited, *Catalogue 161: Oscar Wilde: Manuscripts, Autograph Letters, First Editions* (London, 1929), p. 126. How it came into the possession of either Ross, Millard or Vyvyan Holland is not known, but it may have originally been sold, along with the rest of Wilde's library, on 24 April 1895, at the public auction of Wilde's household goods – perhaps as part of lot 30, which included 'a parcel of pamphlets' ('*[Tite Street] Catalogue...*', (London, 1895), p. 5).

62. *Complete Letters*, p. 348.

63. If Wilde was unable to secure a place at dinner he was not the only one, the *PMG* reporting on the day of the dinner that 'many members have been unable to obtain seats ... the company will number 320, including between forty and fifty MPs – the largest number ever ... at a dinner of the Club.' (*PMG*, 8 May 1888, p. 4.) However, even if Wilde did not dine at Willis's he may have been among the members and guests admitted after dinner to hear the speeches (the names of such attendees were not included in official lists). Browning, who was a prominent member of the club, was one of the lucky diners on the night.

64. Barry O'Brien, in *The Life of Parnell*, Vol. II (London, 1898), p. 190, wrote of the occasion, 'I doubt if he ever addressed a more sympathetic and even enthusiastic audience .... They were prepared for an advanced policy and an extreme speech. There was not a branch of the National League which would have more readily declared for the Plan of Campaign than the rising young Liberals of the Eighty Club'.

65. *The Times*, 9 May 1888, p. 11.

66. *PMG*, 8 May 1888, p. 4.

67. *Hansard* HC Deb. vol. 313 col. 1225, 18 April 1887. Quoted in *C.S. Parnell*, p. 101.

68. *The Belfast News-Letter*, 5 July 1888, p. 5. Wilde may have known O'Donnell from his mother's salons.

69. *Complete Letters*, p. 369. The sentiments Wilde expressed in his letter to Gladstone echoed an earlier letter he had sent to the Liberal leader which accompanied the gift of his book *The Happy Prince and Other Tales* (1888). 'I should like to have the pleasure of presenting it,' Wilde wrote in June 1888, 'to one whom I, and all who have Celtic blood in their veins, must ever honour and revere, and to whom my country is so deeply indebted.' (*Complete Letters*, p. 350). A few weeks after writing his November letter to Gladstone Wilde attended an Eighty Club at home at the Westminster Palace Hotel in London, along with Haldane and Oscar Browning (*The Standard*, 22 November 1888, p. 5).

70. *Complete Letters*, p. 371. Wilde uses the phrase in a letter to the managing editor of the paper, *The Scots Observer: An Imperial Review*. In replying to an invitation to write for the paper Wilde says (and we quote the original manuscript rather than the published version, in which the punctuation is edited in the interests of

legibility): 'It will give me great pleasure to write for you – but as I am very busy it would be better not to advertise my name as a contributor – Besides I hear your paper is anti-Home rule – and I am a most recalcitrant patriot.' (British Library, Add MS 81699). The adjective 'recalcitrant' has sometimes been interpreted to mean 'reluctant' (e.g. in Clayworth, A., 'Wilde the Irishman: the reclamation of a "recalcitrant patriot"', *The Wildean* 9 (July 1996), p. 28–31.) However, in this context the word 'recalcitrant' can only refer to the intensity of Wilde's nationalist feeling – he is making it clear to the editor of the *Observer* that he is a defiant Home Ruler and obstinately disobedient towards the paper's official political line. The OED definition of 'recalcitrant' can be quoted here: '1. Obstinately disobedient; uncooperative, refractory; objecting to constraint or restriction. "A recalcitrant pin falling from its rightful place" (*Cornhill Magazine*, September 1866). 2. Characterized by obstinacy or refractoriness. "She came in rather a recalcitrant mood, expecting to be patronized" (J. Addams, *Twenty Years at Hull-House*, 1910)'. See also the OED definition of the verb 'recalcitrate': 'to "kick out" *against* or *at* a thing; to show strong objection or repugnance; to manifest vigorous opposition or resistance; to be obstinately disobedient or refractory'.

71. *Freeman's Journal and Daily Commercial Advertiser*, 5 February 1889, p. 5.

72. *Glasgow Herald*, 22 March 1888, p. 7.

73. Lewis was elected as an Eighty Club member on 29 March 1889 (*Account Books* 1889–1892). Wilde's close friendship with Lewis may have given him an insider's insight into the sessions of the Commission; it also provided him with an additional social link to Parnell. For the published account of the proceedings Wilde acquired see Lot 17 of the *[Tite Street] Catalogue ...* (p. 4) which was comprised of 'Parnell Commission, &c., 13 vols.'. A newspaper report of the 1895 sale of Wilde's library and household goods, apparently written by an eye-witness, notes that 'Thirteen volumes of the Parnell Commission were sold' (*West London Press, Westminster and Chelsea News,* 26 April 1895). The publication in question may have been the multi-volume government Blue Book published on the commission, or *Parnellism and Crime: The Special Commission Reprinted from 'The Times'* which was published in 35 parts in 1888–90. Wilde also appears to have owned a pen and ink portrait of Pigott, forger of the 'Parnell' letters, done by Frank Lockwood, one of the barristers at the

Commission. (*A Catalogue of select books, letters and manuscripts from the private library of Richard Le Gallienne.* Anderson Auction Company (New York, 1905), p. 70, lot 782.) In an undated letter to Arthur Clifton, Wilde said he felt 'tired' after attending one hearing of the commission. (*Complete Letters*, p. 382.)

74. The sketch was published in *The Graphic* on 16 February 1889, accompanying a short article reviewing the sessions during the second week of that month.

75. *Freeman's Journal and Daily Commercial Advertiser*, 21 February 1889, p. 5. At a session two days later Wemyss Reid produced evidence which materially helped Parnell (see *The Daily Chronicle*, 23 February 1889.)

76. Reports on 9 March 1889 in *The Times*, p. 12, and the *PMG*, p. 7. Birrell would be Chief Secretary for Ireland from 1907 to 1916, resigning after the 1916 Easter Rising.

77. The esteem in which Wilde was held by the club's hierarchy is confirmed by an official Eighty Club letter now in the Harry Ransom Humanities Research Center, University of Texas at Austin (Oscar Wilde Papers; II. Correspondence, 1877–1900); "Eighty" Club--3.7; RLIN Record # TXRC02-A3). Thanks to Gerald Cloud, former Carl and Lily Pforzheimer Curator of Early Books and Manuscripts at the Center, for sending us a copy of this document. The letter, which is addressed to Arthur Clifton, and dated 5 July 1889, confirms that Clifton has been elected as a member of the Eighty Club: 'you were proposed by O. Wilde', it reads, and 'seconded by W.S. Sherrington.'; Wilde and Sherrington have signed the document. The Eighty Club evidently trusted Wilde's judgement and guarantee of Clifton's character, and Wilde was evidently enthusiastic enough about the organization to introduce his friend to it. Clifton, a member of the National Liberal Club, was a solicitor and poet, whose 'delicate ear for music' Wilde admired (*Complete Letters*, p. 375). On 16 August (a few weeks after joining the Eighty) Clifton published a political poem in *The Globe* entitled 'Ballade of Sad Members' which refers to the imprisonment, under the Coercion Act, of the Radical Liberal MP and Eighty Club member, Charles Conybeare, for distributing alms to evicted tenants in Ireland. Sherrington, like Clifton, was a member of the London legal fraternity. We are grateful to Matthew Sturgis for providing information about Clifton, and for identify-

ing him as the candidate Wilde proposed for Eighty Club membership.

78. This is how the room was described in an account of a later Eighty Club meeting (*PMG*, June 26 1890, p. 4), and in an illustration of the Marquis of Ripon giving a speech to the Eighty Club at the hotel, published in the *Daily Graphic*, 30 November 1892. The number of guests is recorded in the official history of the Eighty Club (*The Eighty Club 1880–1955: Seventy Five Years of Service* (London, 1955), p. 3). The average attendance for such gatherings was between 100 and 200.

79. *The Times*, 11 April 1889, p. 8; see also the *Daily News*, 11 April 1889, p. 5, and *The Sheffield & Rotherham Independent*, 11 April 1889, pp. 4 & 5.

80. Wilde's article was printed on 13 April (*Journalism II*, pp. 203–206). We wonder whether the Eighty Club hierarchy would have regarded such anti-coercion comments as examples of the 'political work for the [Liberal] party' Wilde had promised to carry out on joining the club. Soon after his speech Wilde renewed his membership of the club and preserved his receipt for the one guinea annual subscription (dated 26 April 1889) between the pages of his copy of *The Eighty Club 1891* (London, 1891) now in the Clark Library (PR5828.E34).

Wilde's payment was also recorded in the Eighty Club account book. The club's eaccount books for 1889–1892 and 1893–1896 are now in the Bodleian Library (MS. Eng. d. 2017–8). Thomas Wright would like to thank Michael Richardson and Ian Coates of Special Collections, University of Bristol Library, for information regarding the Eighty Club papers and Colin Harris, Superintendent Special Collections Reading Rooms, The Bodleian Library Oxford, for allowing him access to them.

81. *The Cambridge Independent Press*, 23 November 1888, p. 6. We recall that the Eighty Club was formed partly in order to provide speakers at political events throughout England, organized by local Liberal groups such as the CULC, and that it was the duty of club members to speak at these meetings. *The Eighty Club 1890* records that 'the number of speeches made during the year [i.e. 1889] by members of the club has been 653.' It confirms that 'meetings were held' at the 'Cambridge University Liberal Club' (pp. 9–11).

82. *Complete Letters*, p. 407.

83. Wilde, Monkswell and Browning later attended a meeting of the Society of Authors together (*The Daily News*, 17 July 1891, p. 6).

84. Wilde's speech at the CULC is described on the website of the Keynes Society (Alumni Society of the Cambridge Student Liberal Democrats), edited by Seth Thévoz (see especially http://keynessociety.wordpress.com/?s=Wilde). A reference to it also appears in Thévoz's article on the history of the CULC, '1886–1916: The birth and growth of Cambridge University Liberal Club', *Journal of Liberal History* 91 (Summer 2016), pp. 10-22 (especially p. 15). Thévoz's account of the CULC is based on various sources, such as the *Cambridge University Liberal Club minutebook 1886–97*, Montagu MSS AS4/1/1, Wren Library, Trinity College, Cambridge. Thévoz discovered the reference to Wilde's Cambridge talk among the research papers of the late Prof. Peter Calvert of the University of Southampton, who was compiling a history of the CULC. These papers are now in Thévoz's possession. We gratefully acknowledge Thévoz's help with our account of the Cambridge meeting.

85. *PMG*, 29 May 1889, p. 6.

86. *Northern Echo*, 2 August 1889, p. 4; and *The Times*, 1 August 1889, p. 7. Constance Wilde had, for sometime, been active in party politics, joining the Women's Liberal Association (WLA), and bringing her husband along to many of its dinners and conversaziones, some of which had Irish and Home Rule themes (see *PMG*, 7 March 1888, p. 3; *PMG*, 17 April 1888, p. 8; and *Daily News*, 30 April 1888, p. 6). The Wildes again attended a WLA 'Home Rule party', a week or so later, which was a more formal affair, with several speeches being given on Ireland. In one of these speeches a Liberal MP condemned coercion; in another Justin McCarthy, one of several Irish MPs present, argued 'with great force, amid the warmly expressed sympathy of the company' that 'Gladstone's proposal alone could permanently settle the Irish question.' While the speeches were being given the guests signed an 'address of sympathy with the Irish people' (*Daily News*, 30 April 1888, p. 6). In May 1889 Constance gave a paper on Irish politics to the WLA. In a speech characterised by 'earnestness' and 'ease', Constance stressed the benefits of Home Rule (*Northern Echo*, 24 May 1889, p. 4; *Daily News*, 24 May 1889, p. 6; and *PMG*, 24 May 1889, p. 6). It is worth noting in passing here that Lady Chiltern (wife of the politician-hero of Wilde's *An Ideal Husband*), is a WLA member.

87. William and Catherine Gladstone's autographs are dated 'Easter Eve 1888' [i.e. 31 March 1888] (Cox, D. (ed.), *Constance Wilde's Autograph*

Book 1886–1896 (London, 2022), pp. 86–87). Gladstone's diary for this date shows he spent the evening at Aston Clinton (Bucks), the seat of Louisa, dowager Lady de Rothschild. Perhaps he met the Wildes at a gathering there. In March 1888 Constance told a friend that she had seen a 'good deal' of Gladstone at 'political parties'.
F. Moyle, *Constance: The Tragic and Scandalous Life of Mrs Oscar Wilde* (London, 2011), p. 148.

88. Wilde would dedicate his fairy tales 'The Birthday of the Infanta' and 'The Star-Child' to Mrs Grenfell and to Asquith's future wife Margot Tennant, when they were published in *A House of Pomegranates* (1891). Robert Ross may have been referring to Wilde's social success in Liberal social circles when he wrote 'it was ... in political and social centres that Wilde's amazing powers were rightly appreciated and where he was welcomed as the most brilliant of living talkers'. (*Reviews*, p. xii.) For an account of *The Speaker* dinner see the *PMG*, 18 December 1889, p. 6, and *Journalism I*, p. xlii. Wilde also seems to have visited the National Liberal Club, to meet his friend Arthur Clifton, who was a member (see *Complete Letters*, p. 410). Clifton had joined the National Liberal Club as a London-based member in 1885. (7 June 2014 email from Michael Meadowcroft, Hon. Archivist, National Liberal Club to Thomas Wright).

89. These men were present together at a political conversazione in Kensington at which Mrs Gladstone spoke (*PMG*, 30 April 1888, p. 10). Wilde was also on first name terms with McCarthy's son, the MP and Eighty Club member Justin H. McCarthy (see *Complete Letters*, p. 399). James Carew's wife Helen would become one of Wilde's posthumous benefactors, paying for his monument in Père Lachaise Cemetery.

90. O'Connor, Mrs T.P., *I Myself* (London, 1910), p. 159. Mrs T.P. writes of their meeting, 'Mr Wilde said my vernacular proclaimed me Irish. I told him, however, that I had no Irish blood, but was of French extraction, and he said that was the next best thing.'

91. Ibid., p. 224.

92. *St. Paul Daily News*, 10 August 1889, p. 3.

93. The inscription is dated 24 July 1888 (*Constance Wilde's Autograph Book 1886–1896*, pp. 88–89). A few days previously Constance had participated in an Irish 'fancy fair' at Olympia with Mrs T.P., Mrs Gladstone and Miss McCarthy. The fair was organized to promote the Irish

lace industry and as part of the Home Rule propaganda campaign. Constance wore 'a necklace of green shamrocks' and among the items she sold was the portrait of Parnell. (*PMG*, 18 July 1888, p. 5). Men such as O'Connor and McCarthy are examples of what Roy Foster has called 'micks on the make' – Irishmen of talent who migrated to England in the late nineteenth century and 'made a good thing out of it'. (*Paddy and Mr Punch*, p. 282.) Wilde of course was one of the most celebrated examples of the group, with the difference that he did not, like the two politicians just named, hail from the 'aspiring Catholic middle classes of provincial Victorian Ireland' (Ibid., p. 290), but rather from the Dublin Protestant professional middle class (and indeed from a family that aspired to minor Anglo-Irish gentry status). Wilde presumably felt at home in the company of middle-class Catholic Irish MPs, in an alien English context, because of shared nationality; the 'marginalization and duality' (Ibid., p. 296.) of his social position within Ireland was less of an issue in England, where every member of the group would have been identified (by the English and presumably by each other) as Irish. This may, in turn, help account for the ease with which Wilde used the words 'We Irish' in England and the relish with which he paraded his Irishness. For example Yeats remarked on the way Wilde 'commended and dispraised himself … by attributing characteristics like his own to his country: "We Irish are too poetical to be poets; we are a nation of brilliant failures, but we are the greatest talkers since the Greeks."' (*Autobiographies*, p. 135). In a review of a Wilde book, published in Parnell's *United Ireland*, Yeats commented: 'much about [Wilde] is Irish of the Irish. I see in his life and works an extravagant Celtic crusade against Anglo-Saxon stupidity…' (*United Ireland*, 26 September 1891, p. 5.) Likewise, Wilde emphasized his Irishness in his exchanges with George Bernard Shaw, suggesting their plays formed a 'Hibernian school' (*Complete Letters*, p. 563); Shaw in turn spoke of Wilde as 'acutely' Irish and, as such, incomprehensible to the English. Vincent O'Sullivan, an Irish-American who hailed from Catholic middle-class Kerry stock, provides further testimony. In O'Sullivan's company Wilde spoke of 'the insolence with which the English have always treated us', and criticised the English for looking down on the Irish because they were a 'Catholic race'. O'Sullivan regarded Wilde as 'very Irish in aspect and methods', comparing him to 'Burke, Congreve, Steele, Sheridan' (*Aspects of Wilde*, p. 79).

On the other hand, differences of class (and to a lesser extent of religion) among the London Irish are detectable beneath the surface. This is evident from Shaw's memoir 'Memories of Oscar Wilde'. Shaw, who hailed from the Protestant lower middle-class (as opposed to the upper middle-class or aspiring minor gentry class of the Wildes), repeatedly condemns Wilde as a 'Dublin Snob' who vulgarly snubbed men out of 'odious class feeling'. As an example he cites something Wilde 'wrote about T.P. O'Connor with deliberate, studied, wounding insolence, with his Merrion Square Protestant pretentiousness in full cry against the Catholic'. (Shaw is presumably referring to the letters Wilde wrote to the *PMG* about O'Connor, published in the paper on 20 September 1894, p. 3, and 25 September 1894, p. 3, and repr. in *Complete Letters*, p. 611 & pp. 613-615; it should be noted, however, that Wilde's antagonism towards O'Connor may also have had a political source, as T.P. had turned against Parnell, in the wake of the O'Shea divorce scandal at the end of 1890). Intriguingly, Shaw suggests that 'this ... sort of folly' prevented Wilde from 'laying any solid social foundations' in London, and that this contributed indirectly to his downfall. (Shaw's 'Memories' are reproduced in a separately numbered sequence of pages after p. 548 in Harris, F., *Oscar Wilde: His Life and Confessions* (New York, 1916), Vol. II; the above quotations appear on pp. 16-19 of 'Memories').

94. *Complete Letters*, p. 421.

95. *Bibliography of Oscar Wilde*, p. 237.

96. *PMG*, 26 June 1890, p. 4.

97. Foster, R.F., *Modern Ireland 1600-1972* (London, 1988), p. 424.

98. Interestingly one of these criticisms appeared in the anti-Home Rule paper *The Scots Observer* and may have been, in part, politically motivated. The paper described Wilde's story an offence to 'public morals' and suggested that it dealt 'with matters only fitted for the Criminal investigation department' (*Scots Observer*, 5 July 1890, p. 181.) Wilde defended his novel in a letter that was published in the *Scots Observer* on 12 July 1890, p. 201-202(repr. in *Complete Letters*, pp. 438-439). Wilde's defence in turn provoked a series of letters (by various hands) on the subject of the relationship between art and morality. One of these (penned by a *Scots Observer* journalist called 'H' and published on 26 July 1890), considered the question of whether critics ought to concentrate on the stylistic or the moral aspects of a work of art. In the course of his discussion 'H' used as an illustration the case of a critic reviewing a

public performance of the song 'God Save Ireland' (the national anthem of nationalists at the end of the nineteenth century). It would be the 'duty of the critic', 'H' argued, to focus on the song's subject, rather than its style, and to attack this 'blackguard doggerel about three cowardly murderers' as 'disgraceful and treasonable' (pp. 253-254.)

Wilde made a point of singling out this remark in a reply to the *Scots Observer*, published on 16 August 1890; he said it was tantamount to a proposal 'that the test of art should be the political opinions of the artist, and that if one differed from the artist on the best way of misgoverning Ireland, one should always abuse his work' (p. 333; repr. in *Complete Letters*, p. 449).

In considering the political subtext to Wilde's treatment by *The Scots Observer* we should recall that he had previously declared his strong opposition to the paper's anti-Home rule stance (see note 70), and also that he had recently mocked its editor, W.E. Henley, for having been 'exiled to Scotland to edit a Tory paper' (*Complete Letters*, p. 409). It's also worth mentioning that Wilde's party-political views inform a passage in the first chapter of *The Picture of Dorian Gray* which contains a caricature of a Tory imperialist. In a conversation with Lord Henry Wotton, Basil Hallward describes a party at which the hostess introduces him to 'a most truculent and red-faced old gentleman covered all over with orders and ribbons, and hissing into my ear, in a tragic whisper which must have been perfectly audible to everybody in the room, [she said] something like "Sir Humpty Dumpty–you know–Afghan frontier–Russian intrigues: very successful man–wife killed by an elephant–quite inconsolable–wants to marry a beautiful American widow–everybody does nowadays–hates Mr. Gladstone–but very much interested in beetles: ask him what he thinks of Schouvaloff."' (Bristow, J. (ed.), *The Complete Works of Oscar Wilde, Vol. 3; The Picture of Dorian Gray: The 1890 and 1891 Texts* (Oxford, 2005), 9.27-10.5).

Vincent O'Sullivan remarked of Henley and Wilde that 'Two men more different were never made', citing politics as a key difference: 'Henley's imperialism, patrioteering, waving of the Union-Jack, to Wilde said nothing at all' (*Aspects of Wilde*, p. 94). In this context, we can also quote the anti-Irish comment on Wilde's failed 1895 prosecution of Lord Queensebrry made by Henley's *The National Observer* (successor to *The Scots Observer*). The editor of the paper congratulated the court on 'destroying the ... obscure imposter, whose prominence has been a social outrage ever since he transferred from

Trinity Dublin to Oxford his vices'. When Wilde was convicted of gross indecency, the paper likewise remarked that the sentence 'revealed' him as an Irish 'imposter' who had merely 'aped' English 'civilisation.' (Quoted in 'The Other Addict: Reflections on Colonialism and Oscar Wilde's Opium Smoke Screen', p. 273.)

99. These phrases appear in chapters 12 and 17 of the 1891 version of *The Picture of Dorian Gray* (London, 1891). Wilde is likely to have seen Parnell in part as a victim of English middle-class hypocrisy and prejudice regarding sexual matters. His irritation on this issue had informed the original version of *Dorian Gray*, and may also inform the additions he made for the 1891 book version. As Nicholas Frankel's edition of *Dorian Gray* makes clear, in the original typescript of the novel Wilde challenged English sexual mores, primarily with regard to homosexuality, but also with regard to unconventional heterosexual relationships such as Parnell's and Kitty O'Shea's. In the typescript references are made to Dorian's extra-marital sexual relations with women, and the word 'mistress' is used. (*The Picture of Dorian Gray: An Annotated, Uncensored Edition*, pp. 47-48).

100. *Criticism*, 239.17, 255.22-23, & 255.31-256.9.

101. This idea is also supported by the context in which Wilde's essay appeared. In another article, from the same issue of the *Fortnightly*, there is a direct reference to Parnell ('Public Life and Private Morals', pp. 213-228, see pp. 225-226). In the previous month's issue there had also been a piece entitled 'The Irish Leadership' by Frederic Harrison, (pp. 122-125). Wilde's essay also appeared in the February issue alongside Grant Allen's article 'The Celt in English Art' (pp. 267-277) which discussed the revolutionary influence of the 'Celtic reflux on Teutonic Britain' in the spheres of politics and art: 'The Celt comes back upon us', he wrote, 'with all the Celtic gifts and all the Celtic ideals – imagination, fancy, decorative skill, artistic handicraft; free land, free speech, human equality, human brotherhood'. Allen argues that most prominent radicals are Celts, singling out Michael Davitt, William Morris, Bernard Shaw, Cunninghame-Graham, John Burns, and the leaders of the Plan of Campaign and Home Rule movement. It is no coincidence that Wilde was in contact, at some point in his life, with all of these men; nor, evidently, did Allen consider it as such. In his article he refers to Wilde as an 'Irishman to the core' 'whom

only fools ever mistook for a mere charlatan, and whom wise men know for a man of rare insight and strong common-sense'; he also identifies a connection between 'the decorative revival' with which Wilde was associated, 'and the Celtic upheaval of radicalism and socialism.' On reading the article Wilde wrote to Allen to express the 'real delight' that both he and his mother took in it. 'I was dining', he added, 'at the House of Commons on Thursday, and proposed to some Scotch and Welsh members, who had read your article with pride and pleasure, that ... *all* of us who are Celts ... should inaugurate a Celtic Dinner, and assert ourselves, and show these tedious Angles or Teutons what a race we are, and how proud we are to belong to that race.' (*Complete Letters*, pp. 469–470.) This letter places Wilde right at the centre of London politics, socially as well as geographically.

102. See *Criticism*, pp. 575–576, where Isobel Murray and Linda Dowling are cited. Wilde cannot be referring to Dilke because he criticises journalists who 'invite the public to ... dictate to ... the man['s] party' and 'country'. This comment only makes sense in relation to the Irish Parnell (Dilke was English), whose party and country were being ordered, by Gladstone and British public opinion, to jettison their leader in November–December 1890, the time Wilde was working on his essay (*Criticism*, p. lxx). Moreover, Wilde explicitly criticises journalists who 'at present' (i.e. in the winter of 1890–1891) are attacking 'a great statesman ... a leader of political thought ... a creator of political force.' Dilke was not even an MP at this time, let alone a 'leader' or 'great statesman', while the much-publicised divorce case he'd been involved in had taken place five years previously. In contrast to some of Wilde's editors, historians of Irish politics have read Wilde's reference correctly (e.g. see Callanan, F., *The Parnell Split 1890-91* (Syracuse, 1992), p. 303 n4). Did Wilde's Gladstonian Liberalism inform his political essay? 'The Soul of Man' espoused the eminently Liberal doctrine that the state's principal role was to oversee and facilitate important social activities – such as the appreciation and creation of art, and the expression of each citizen's personality. An initial period of state intervention would, according to Wilde, be necessary to construct a society in which these pursuits could flourish – machines would have to be introduced to carry out all dreary manual labour, working hours would have to be capped, etc. However, even these measures would have been acceptable to some Eighty Clubbers. John Morley had advocated similar policies when he had addressed the club on 'Liberal-

ism and Social reforms' at London's St. James's Hall on 19 November 1889. The measures he proposed that evening included the state provision of food, education and housing, and a reduction of labour hours allowing workers more leisure to read. Among Morley's audience at St. James's Hall sat Oscar Wilde (*The Times*, 20 November 1889, p. 9) In early 1890, Wilde would, in addition, have received the club's verbatim report of Morley's speech (*Liberalism & Social Reforms, 19th November, 1889. Speech by John Morley* (London, 1890)). When he sat down to write 'The Soul of Man' in 1890 for the *Fortnightly* (which Morley had, incidentally, once edited) it is possible then that Wilde recalled Morley's words, as there are a number of echoes between the two texts. For example, both texts open with a discussion of the nature of Socialism, and clarify what the respective authors mean by the word. Both speak of the precarious nature of manual work under capitalism – Morley writing of the way 'the workman's life is at the mercy of the ebbs and flows of the market' (*Liberalism & Social Reforms*, p. 28), and Wilde celebrating the fact that, under socialism, 'If a frost comes we shall not have a hundred thousand men out of work' (*Criticism*, 232.24-25). Both suggest workers should have leisure to read (*Liberalism & Social Reforms*, p. 25; *Criticism*, 247.9-11); and Wilde remarked that 'There is no doubt at all that this is the future of machinery, and just as trees grow while the country gentleman is asleep, so while Humanity will be amusing itself, or enjoying cultivated leisure – which, and not labour, is the aim of man – or making beautiful things, or reading beautiful things, or simply contemplating the world with admiration and delight, machinery will be doing all the necessary and unpleasant work.' Finally, both use the phrase 'against human nature' – Morley suggests that a Socialist society run by the state is against human nature (p. 13) while Wilde remarks of the society he is adumbrating: 'It will, of course, be said that such a scheme as is set forth here is quite unpractical, and goes against human nature. This is perfectly true. It is unpractical, and it goes against human nature.' (*Criticism*, 262.24-26.)

103. Wilde paid his subs on the following dates: 11 April 1891, 5 January 1892, 10 July 1893 and 3 November 1894. The Club *Account Books* for 1889-1892 and 1893-1896 (Bodleian Library, Mss. Eng. d. 2017-8).

104. *The Times*, 3 December 1890, p. 11.

105. Sir Henry James at a meeting of the Liberal Union Club, 16 December

1890, as reported in *The Times* the following day (p. 9).

106. Yeats' response to Parnell's fall is suggestive in this context: 'when Parnell fell from power in 1891,' he wrote, 'A disillusioned and embittered Ireland turned from parliamentary politics.' (*Autobiographies*, p. 554.) Owen Dudley Edwards makes a number of illuminating remarks on Wilde's response to Parnell's fall: Wilde, he comments, 'missed few opportunities for cool and deadly thrusts against Parnell's enemies [i.e. Balfour and Froude] ... but when Parnell's fall dashed Wilde's hopes he reacted with the white heat of so many other literary Parnellites. Domiciled in England, he denounced the hypocrisy of English journalism where the youthful Joyce in Ireland mourned Parnell's martyrdom at the hands of the pusillanimous Irish. The Parnell movement itself symbolised Wilde's larger conflict of past and future: he hailed its modernism, above all in the American character it had now assumed ... yet it was part of what Yeats and Lady Wilde exhibited in their rediscovery of Celtic mythology ... the Irish political success [i.e. of the years 1886–1891] ... was an inspirational music in the background of Wilde's own cultural embattlement. Shaw, Yeats, Wilde, even Joyce, all became their own Parnells, most conspicuously in Wilde's case with his own triumph and disaster in the years immediately after Parnell's fall.' (Dudley Edwards, O. (ed.), *The Fireworks of Oscar Wilde* (London, 1989), p. 31.) The publication of 'The Soul of Man' may also have been one of the factors in Wilde's apparent loss of interest in the Eighty Club. For all its radical Liberal resonances, the essay contained revolutionary passages that may have raised the eyebrows of some of the club's conservative members. In celebrating political agitation, individualism, and art as 'disturbing and disintegrating' forces of 'immense value' (*Criticism*, 250.23–24), it revealed Wilde as, in Alfred Douglas' words, 'a mild Liberal by pretention but a rebel at heart' (Lord Alfred Douglas, *Oscar Wilde and Myself*, (London), p. 61). Its subversive tone apparently did Wilde 'a greater disservice with the governing classes than anything else he could have said or done.' (Pearson, H., *The Life of Oscar Wilde* (London, 1946), p. 165.)

107. *Constance: The Tragic and Scandalous Life of Mrs Oscar Wilde*, p. 194. Wilde's only recorded comment on Parnell's end was made years after the event to Vincent O'Sullivan. 'There is something vulgar in all success' he said, apropos of Parnell, 'The greatest men fail – or seem to have failed.' (*Aspects of Wilde*, p. 222). Wilde was

echoing here his San Francisco lecture on 'Irish Poets and Poetry of the Nineteenth Century' during which he remarked of Smith O'Brien 'I remember [him] so well ... with ... the sadness of one who had failed – no, perhaps I should not use the word failed, such failures are at least often grander than a hundred victories'. (*Irish Poets and Poetry of the Nineteenth Century*, p. 30.)

108. Ellmann, *Oscar Wilde*, p. 332.

109. *PMG*, 29 June 1892, pp. 1–2, repr. in *Complete Interviews*, Vol. II, pp. 603–606. This carries with it an implicit rejection of the Union of England and Ireland, as Wilde emphasises difference and distance rather than unity and connection between the two cultures.

110. Partridge, J.B., 'A Wilde Idea', *Punch* 103, 9 July 1892, p. 1.

111. The society was founded by Yeats, Charles Gavan Duffy, T.W. Rolleston, Barry O'Brien (all of whom Wilde knew) and Douglas Hyde, future (and first) President of Ireland. Wilde's name appeared in the register as 'Oscar Fingal O'Flaherty Wills Wilde' (*Importance of Being Irish*, p. 188). The society's aims included providing a centre for social and literary intercourse for Irishmen and women in London, and circulating in popular form approved works relating to Irish literature, history and art. Its nationalist ethos is evident in one of the first lectures given under its auspices, by Charles Gavan Duffy, a veteran of '48. (*Glasgow Herald*, 28 July 1892, p. 6.)

112. Wilde's play in some respects mirrored recent Irish political events – it features a prominent MP whose brilliant career is in danger of being ruined by a private scandal. Mrs Cheveley tries to blackmail the progressive Liberal MP Sir Robert Chiltern, threatening to expose a nefarious past action if he refuses to meet her price. 'My dear Sir Robert', she says, 'you [would be] ruined [by exposure]. Remember to what point your Puritanism in England has brought you... You know what your English newspapers are like.... Think of their loathsome joy, of the delight they would have in dragging you down .... Think of the hypocrite with his greasy smile penning his leading article.' There is an obvious echo here of Wilde's reference to Parnell in 'The Soul of Man'.

113. Ellmann, *Oscar Wilde*, p. 378. Wilde's remark is perhaps not altogether facetious, since he believed that the Celt would one day rule England through his dominance in art and culture. The fact the Wildes brought their son up to be a fierce nationalist is

eloquent of strong views strongly held within the family.

114. Donohue, J. (ed.), *The Complete Works of Oscar Wilde, Vol. 10: Plays, Vol. 3: The Importance of Being Earnest; 'A Wife's Tragedy' (fragment)* (Oxford, 2019), 781.446-449. This exchange is not only (or indeed principally) a joke aimed at political hypocrisy generally, as is suggested, for instance in *The Picture of Dorian Gray* (Bristow, p. 431). Wilde is in fact making a specific point by ridiculing the Liberal Unionists and indicating the condescension of the Tories towards them (i.e. they are permitted to attend large parties but not invited to dinner). Being a Liberal Unionist is, according to Wilde, tantamount to having 'no politics', and having 'no politics' is an attitude consistent with Jack's general ignorance (a few lines earlier in the play he admits to 'knowing nothing'). For this joke Wilde used one of his many epigrammatic formulae. Sometime previously he had been asked by Arthur Balfour what his religion was. 'Well, you know', Wilde replied, 'I don't think I have any. I am an Irish Protestant.' (*Aspects of Wilde*, p. 65.) The political thrust of both remarks is the same, as Balfour championed the rights of the Protestant Unionist minority in Ireland.

Balfour touched on Irish politics, indirectly, when he met Constance Wilde on 2 August 1891, and wrote in her autograph book. Underneath an inscription penned by T.P. O'Connor (see p. 48 above), Balfour wrote: 'Of all exercise of the human intelligence Political Prophecy is the most vain. Arthur James Balfour 2.8.91.' (*Constance Wilde's Autograph Book 1886-1896*, pp. 88-89.) Clear-sighted, but somewhat short-sighted, Balfour was right in so far as Ireland did not achieve Home Rule in the 1890s, but many men of O'Connor's generation did live to see the establishment of the Irish Free State in 1922, which was an important step towards the creation of an independent Irish republic. It is perhaps significant that the Wildes' encounters with Balfour featured Irish politics; it is also interesting that the Wildes socialized with Tories as well as Liberals.

115. A comment Wilde made about his conviction suggests an awareness of the possible connection or symmetry between sexual behaviour and Irish politics: 'A patriot put in prison for loving his country', he wrote in 1898 after his release, 'loves his country, and a poet in prison for loving boys loves boys'. (*Complete Letters*, p. 1019.)

116. *Oscar Wilde: His Life and Confessions*, Vol. I, p. 279. It is interesting, in this context, to see how the *Freeman's Journal and Daily Commercial Adver-*

tiser coverage of the conclusion of Wilde's trials (27 May 1895, p. 6) is 'informed by "an anti-imperialist discourse"' (Walshe, E., *Oscar's Shadow: Wilde, Homosexuality and Modern Ireland* (Cork, 2012), p. 15).

117. *Complete Letters*, p. 769.

118. For a full account of Wilde's arrest and subsequent trials, and of the possible Liberal conspiracy, see the Introduction to Holland, M. (ed.), *Irish Peacock & Scarlet Marquess: The Real Trial of Oscar Wilde* (London, 2003), which we have drawn on here, and Bristow, J., *Oscar Wilde on Trial: The Criminal Proceedings, from Arrest to Imprisonment* (New Haven & London, 2022), especially pp. 99–101.

119. Healy, T.M., *Letters and Leaders of my Day*, Vol. II (London, 1928), p. 416.

120. Marjoribanks, E., *The Life of Lord Carson*, Vol. I (London, 1932), p. 230. This analysis of events may have come from Carson or a source within the Marjoribanks family. Carson's biographer Edward Marjoribanks was the nephew of the Liberal MP Edward Marjoribanks (Lord Tweedmouth from 1894), a member of Rosebery's Cabinet from 1894 to 1895, and the Vice President of the Eighty Club who presided over the 1889 club conversazione at which Wilde had proposed a vote of thanks.

121. Haldane, R., *Autobiography* (London, 1929), p. 166. Haldane incorrectly recalls that he visited Wilde at Holloway; the visit took place on 12 June, by which time Wilde was at Pentonville. See also Haldane's letters to the Governors of Pentonville and Wandsworth prisons, and to Ruggles-Brise, Chairman of the Prison Commission (Prison Commission file 8/432, Public Records Office).

122. Dudley Edwards, O., 'The Soul of Man under Hibernicism', *Irish Studies Review* 11 (summer 1995), p. 13.